Israel Behind Bars

Maximum Security
Maximum Hope

Israel Behind Bars

Maximum Security
Maximum Hope

Rabbi Major Fishel Jacobs

Jacobs Media International Inc.

New York

Published by Jacobs Media International Inc.

Mailing address:

Box 68

383 Kingston Avenue

Brooklyn, New York 11213

This is a work of nonfiction. However, some names of inmates and staff, as well as any identifying information have been deleted or altered. This is, of course, for privacy and in some cases security concerns.

ISBN # 0-9776736-0-X

This book is available at special quantity discounts for bulk purchases for sales promotions, fund raising, or educational purposes. Book excerpts or special editions can be created for special needs. For details write: publisher@IsraelBehindBars.com, or call: 1 (212) 655-9278

Printed in the U.S.A.

Praise For

Israel Behind Bars

"We sincerely believe in each individual's ability to draw on inner strength and travel the road to self-improvement. To this end we devote great resources, which can clearly be seen in Rabbi Jacobs' book."

—Colonel Ofer Laufer, *Spokesman of the Israeli Prison Service*

"One of Israel's most unique and powerful personalities, Major Jacobs delivers a sparkling, unforgettable work; one which opens a window to the social history of Israel *amidst* the anguish and struggles of prison life. Inspiring! Brilliant! A must read!"

—Professor Richard Sugarman, *University of Vermont*

"Having worked with Major Jacobs for the past five years in Nitzan Prison, I can testify to the genuineness and authenticity of the interpersonal interactions described in his book. He powerfully brings forth the humanity within 'the walls of despair.' I can also testify that Jacobs' humor is not confined to the written word. He is well known in the prison not only as an officer and rabbi but as a humorist and karate expert as well! I highly recommend this book."

—Joshua M. Weiss, Ph.D., *Dept. of Criminology, Bar-Ilan University*

Dedicated to my mother, for her encouragement.

And, to my father, who loved the manuscript.

Prisoner's Prayer

Master of the Universe!
Free me from this confinement
to a good and peaceful life.
My soul is tired of prison!
Just as You received Noah's prayers—
releasing him, his wife, sons, daughters-in-law
and their possessions from the Ark—
Answer me and take me out of this prison
to the good and gracious life.
I will praise Your name forever.
Amen.

Let it be Your will.

from *The Finder of Life*
Rabbi Chaim Plag'i (1788 - 1868)

Acknowledgments

I would like to take this opportunity to thank the following. (I apologize for not mentioning some of you by rank, it's just too confusing.)

To Hanna Nitzon of the Israel Prison Service Spokesman's office for sincere encouragement. Thank you for all your help along the way.

I want to extend a very warm thank you to the current Spokesman, Ofer Laufer. Your enthusiasm is wonderful. I want to thank you, of course including your wonderful staff, for not only helping this book, but for winning much deserved admiration for the service at large. Your work is inspiring.

I wish to express my appreciation to all the staff members with whom I have worked throughout the years. It was long hours, hard work—but deep friendship. Though there are simply too many to even begin recording all their names, I must mention a few. Mirel for taking me under your wing; Emil and Sarit for helping me prepare the yearly stat-report (at the last minute) and keeping me posted. The security staff is always thanking *me* for filling in when manpower is thin—it is likewise. To all the rest, I extend a heartfelt thank you.

   I would like to thank my last vice-warden, Ilan, for friendship.

   To Dr. Weiss for encouragement and much insight.

   Thank you to the office of the legal advisor.

   I am grateful to all the wardens under whom I served. I'll just note a few: To Shlomi, for the meaning of professionalism; Gabizon for the good-natured atmosphere; Ze'evi for the humility; Yaakov for covering for me; Miki for the personal-style leadership; Yisroel for perspective. From each of you I learned a lot and gained as an officer and as a person.

   I believe that the Commissioners of Prison, who led the entire service during my enlistment, were all exemplary, each in their own right. Arie Bibi from whom I received rank, Amos Azani, (Mrs.) Orit Adato. And, currently, Yaakov Granot who has served during a period of extreme instability throughout the Middle East, not excluding Israel. To be so successful with such grace is amazing.

   Over the years, large numbers of volunteers helped bring all my activities and programs to fruition. It is not possible to mention them all. I would, however, like to take this opportunity to thank all those from the Chabad-Lubavitch movement. As always, you brought much joy to many, as you do worldwide.

Thank you to the editors of the various magazines worldwide who, over the years, carried excerpts from the manuscript-in-progress.

Thank you to our photographer, Debbie Zimelman, for some wonderful shots.

Thanks to my son, Joseph, for critical assistance in various stages of development production.

To my brother, Yisroel, for the nods of approval.

To my editors, Joseph Israel and Sarah Esther Crispe.

To Peggy Whiteneck, for final-touch literary assistance.

To Mom, for all her support.

To Dr. Elka Pinson for graphic layout and critical design advice.

To my wife, Miriam, for everything.

To our children, for patience with their father—while he wrote another book.

Contents

Part II MAXIMUM HOPE

INTRODUCTION

"Whoa! You work in a *prison*," someone says, "I can't *believe* that. What do you *do* there?"

"Well, I..."

"That's so *intense*," they continue. "Isn't it *scary?* They're so *dangerous*..."

"It's not so..."

"How many prisoners are there? That is so *intense*. Do you carry a gun...?"

"Hold off, "I was saying," it's not so..."

"All those walls. You actually have contact with *prisoners?* Aren't you afraid? Have you ever been *attacked?*"

"One second, let me explain..."

I've noticed that people are fascinated by my working in prison. Everyone who hears about it has to know about it. I can understand why. There's a fascination with the unknown: What really goes on in there? Most people have probably never even seen a prison. The government usually builds them out of sight.

England actually founded Australia as an island for convicts on January 26, 1788—the date Captain Arthur Phillip landed there with a thousand sailors, of whom 717 were convicts. In the U.S., Alcatraz Federal Prison, the Rock, was erected out in the *middle* of San Francisco Bay. America's largest maximum-security penitentiary, Angola Prison, population five thousand, is located on eighteen thousand acres of land in Louisiana—blocked in on three sides by the huge Mississippi River, on the fourth by the Tunica Hills. The place most associated in the American mind with prison was situated way up on the Hudson River, the euphemism, "up the river" referred to boating inmates there, near the municipality of Sing Sing.

On approaching a prison, one feels an unnerving trepidation. Layers of barricades vacuum seal the whole works. Everything, everyone outside is out. Everything, everyone inside is in.

Armed vehicle patrols, trained dogs, concertina wire, thick concrete walls, surveillance systems, indiscernible guards up in watchtowers. Uniformed guards watching over a sea of men, each one individually identified by a computer-generated inmate ID number, and pacing to-and-fro in exercise yards. Intermingling, chain-smoking, whispering.

Life behind bars is *not* a storybook. It is *not* fiction. It *is* real flesh and blood people interacting with one another. It is dynamic. Staff work there, many until their retirement. Prisoners live there, many for the majority of their lives. And, by the way, not all men do adapt equally. There are all kinds. They do all kinds of things. Some pace. Some cook. Some play backgammon all day. Some enjoy prison life. Others release energy by self-imposed regimens of exercise and sweat. Some pray. Some write home. Some never adapt at all. There's always at least one guy standing for hours staring out of the bars of his cell window.

As microcosms of society, prisons tend to be ethnically diverse. This diversity complicates an already complex situation. In Israel, as in the Middle East at large, this diversity has a heavy immediacy. Serving time in Israeli prisons are Russian inmates who, ironically, escaped decades of national internment until Communism's fall in the 80s and 90s. Waves of illegal workers, seeking a better life—from the Philippines, Thailand, Romania—are held for extradition by immigration officials. The local criminal element is composed of its own ethnic makeup: Moroccan, Georgian, Yemenite. And, of course, there are around three thousand terrorists—AKA security prisoners—members of Hamas, Jihad, Hizbalah, the Popular Front, all roaming these same buildings.

As an aside, I am aware that some people will be hoping to find in this book details in the treatment of terrorists which will be incriminating to the Israel prison service. They will be disappointed and will need to look elsewhere. In my experience, the overall professional and dignified *modus operandi* conveyed in these chapters applies to all prisoners—without exception. Frankly, I find reports of the mistreatment of such prisoners to be inaccurate and transparent in their motive.

Universally, the reality is that prisons hold people against their will. In any country, at any period of history, that is not a "natural" state for human beings. That's not meant to be a political statement about the institution of incarceration or possible alternatives. It's simply stating the obvious. The Almighty created humans as productive. By definition, much of this is stifled by prison life. Energy stuffed up, builds up.

Am I a liberal or a conservative? I don't think in those terms. I am a realist, and everything I'm reporting is what I saw. I have no agenda. What you will get out of my book, if you read it well, is that life behind bars is about people.

I was born in Brooklyn, New York. On both sides, my grandparents were Jewish immigrants from Russia, Romania, Poland. They spoke mainly Yiddish.

For business purposes, my dad moved the family to New England, where I was raised through high school in a quaint village, population 1,500, called South Royalton, Vermont. My adolescence included skiing, snowmobiling, flying planes, horseback riding (we owned twelve horses).

And, under the direction of world renowned Grandmaster Dr. Tae Yun Kim, I won many regional karate championships, including the 1976 Y.M.C.A. Mid-Atlantic Black Belt Heavyweight fighting title. This fact tied in later to my prison service. From 2001-2003, acquiescing to an official request, and in addition to my chaplaincy duties, I taught fitness and hand-to-hand combat to the prison service staff.

I graduated from the University of Vermont, after which a desire to explore my own heritage took me to Israel, where I spent fourteen years in rabbinical school.

There, under the personal directives of the Lubavitcher Rebbe, Rabbi Menachem Schneersohn, I received ordination from the two head rabbis of Israel, completed studies as a Rabbinic attorney, and eventually published numerous books on practical Jewish law that are in use worldwide.

From August 1992 until June 2005, I worked with the Israeli prison service. In practical terms, this meant wearing uniform and rank (mine was Major) inside the world's most maximum security prisons, nine and a half hours a day, five days a week.

The Prison Service is a branch of the overall Israeli security, working hand in hand with the other arms of internal and external security forces. I was also the first full time chaplain for Israel's only women's prison, Neve Tirzah.

It's no secret: Israel is engulfed in security, economic and regional problems that countries a hundred times its size and age never have to deal with. This affects everyone.

Yet despite typical budget strains and the stress of professional demands, I served with some of the most capable, compassionate men and women I could ever hope to meet. I learned a lot from my service. And I am thankful for it.

PART 1
MAXIMUM SECURITY

1

Ending Up In Jail

"Hey, you want a job in a prison?"

"A *what?*"

"A prison. You know, where they keep prisoners. Guards, barbed wire fences and stuff."

Is this guy kidding? I thought.

The guy on the other end of the phone was an old friend. Eitan Adam, like me, Brooklyn, N.Y. born was working as a medic in a maximum security prison, a fifteen minute drive from my home. It was June, 1992.

"Look, government jobs pay well," he continued, "civil servant perks and all that. The prison where I'm working is looking for rabbis."

The idea was farfetched, out of left field. But my wife,

Miriam, and I had been struggling for over eleven years on her high school teacher's salary and the small student stipend I got compensating for my studies. We were spent emotionally as well as financially. A source of income was clearly needed.

"Give me your I.D. number," he continued. "I'll tell the prison rabbi to get you a one-day entrance pass."

"What am I supposed to do?"

"Come, give a small talk, let them get to know you."

"Them?"

"The prisoners."

"The *pri...*?"

"Fishel, for crying out loud! I'm not talking Chinese here. Get me the number!"

As a teenager, I'd worked in my dad's factory during summer breaks, helping his carpenters construct houses for rentals and, at times, I did other types of physical work for pocket money. Frankly, I had no clue where I'd start earning a living in a foreign country.

Like most people, I'd never seen a prison up close, *definitely* not from inside. But, it somehow seemed predetermined that my life would be full of exciting opportunities; working in a prison would certainly never be monotonous.

Why not? I thought.

A few days later, I found myself facing the entrance to the

largest, most infamous, *foreboding*, bastilles in Israel, Ayalon
Prison in Ramleh, a 25-minute drive from Tel Aviv.

Unbeknownst to me at the time, quite a few colorful
"personalities" decorated its landscape. Hertzel Aviton, for example.
Branded by the media, sealed by history as Israel's most famous and
dangerous criminal, he was serving *multiple* life sentences for a
number of hands-on, cold-blooded murders, including that of *his
own warden. That* on the *lam.*

Under heavily armed guard he'd been granted a compassion
leave to visit his "ailing" father at his apartment. (The sickness was
subsequently widely viewed as concocted.) He slipped out the
bathroom window, climbed three stories down a rope prepared for
this purpose and sped away in a waiting getaway car. It was 7:00 on

Sunday morning, December 13, 1981. Waiting, stalking his warden, Major Roni Nitzon, on his way to work, Aviton stuck his Uzi machine gun into his warden's face, riddling his head, neck, and upper torso with *twenty-one* bullets.

Ami Popper was also serving multiple life sentences for seven fatal shootings. John Demjanjuk, the Cleveland auto worker labeled "Ivan the Terrible," accused of personally running the gas chambers at Treblinka where over 800,000 Jews were murdered, had been held there. So, too, had convicted Nazi war criminal, Adolph Eichmann, executed by hanging on May 31, 1962, his cremated ashes then spread over the Mediterranean Sea. Proud to the very end, without a smudge of remorse, he was quoted in the November, 1960 *Life* magazine interview, entitled "Eichmann's Confession," as saying, "Were we successful in murdering *all* 10,300,00 Jews, my position would have been, 'Excellent. We've eradicated an enemy.'"

Imagine working in a place where these are the people roaming the halls.

Prisons are unearthly places—I have *never* in my entire life felt more unnerved than I did upon entering this one. The second that three-inch thick metal door slammed, I *knew* I was in prison. No other door in the world sounds like *that*.

A word about prison doors can shed a world of light on prisons themselves. The *doors*, more than any single element, encapsulate the prison experience. They are to prisons what wall-to-wall carpeting is to the interior decoration of a home, lighting to a restaurant, background music to a department store, bedside manner to a physician. They set the tone, express the prison's essence.

Doors, anywhere, have personalities. Fashionable clothing store revolving glass doors whirl gracefully, invitingly. Heavy bank vault doors have a particular resonance, a ring, that says "security." The tin metal sound of car doors says, "I'm not important, just a necessary precaution." A huge, squeaky ancient wooden barn door is rustic, homey. If you listen, you can hear all this, pick up what they're saying.

Prison doors are a class all to themselves. It's not only the ice cold iron-against-iron, door-smashing-door-frame explosion. Not just the thick bolt shooting into place. It's not measurable in decibels, nor frequency—*frequency?* They're banging throughout the building continuously, day in and day out. So what *is* it?

Prison doors *have no soul.* Therefore, their *sound* has no soul.

Their empty reverberation clangs chillingly: "You're trapped. Like an animal. You can't get out. It's not *my* fault you're here. But, there's nothing personal. Nothing. You can stand on your head. Get angry. Violent. Throw a fit. Cry. Whine. Go into contortions. Whatever you want. But—you're here. Not getting out. And there's nothing personal about it. SLAM!"

I was uncomfortable, edgy now, inside the outer perimeter security gate, watching the guard matching my I.D. number against the entrance permit. Some other guys, without uniforms, were milling around. My brain raced. Were these guards... or...?

Confirming my entrance pass took two short minutes—two typically intense, condensed *prison* minutes during which Mr. Guard: 1) sipped a cup of coffee I assumed was *not* hot 2) bit into a sandwich, prepared—sometime 3) returned from the bathroom 4) answered the phone four times 5) casually joked with who-*are*-these-guys-anyhow 6) read the headlines 7) glanced at me 8) scribbled some notes into an official record book.

I stood there, disoriented, my internal electrical circuitry momentarily overloaded.

"Cellular phone, weapon, metal objects?" he monotoned.

"No," I answered, hoping to sound composed, but far from it. I felt like I was taking a physical, naked. Should I smile or what?

"Go through," he said, throwing a bored, routine glance in the direction of the walkthrough metal detector.

Halfway through, the indicator lights began flashing. My heart nearly stopped.

I looked at Mr. Guard. He looked back.

Aha! He caught me, I thought. But I had nothing to catch.

"Okay," he said, "go through." Then answered another phone call.

The anomalous merging of thick, impenetrable, metal-girded concrete walls, incessant slamming metal doors, morose atmosphere, and *nonchalant* behavior is something which will haunt me for the rest of my life.

Inside, I was greeted by Eitan, who led me through an endless, confusing maze of corridors to the chaplain's office. The shepherd of the world's most peculiar flock got right to the point: "Can you give a small talk to some prisoners?"

"Sure," I said, not particularly *sure* about *anything* at this point—images of my reception by Mr. Guard and Unidentified Guys, Inc. still played in my mind.

"Come."

He led me down a two-yard-wide corridor, lined with cell after cell—full of men wearing shorts, sandals or plastic bathroom slippers—lounging, sprawling on bunk beds, watching TV, cooking on small hotplates, playing backgammon (the official prison pastime). We arrived at a 2.5-square-yard cubicle, bare but regularly whitewashed: the ward's synagogue.

Four inmates waited inside, seated on wooden benches. The moment we entered, one left. Got up and left. Nothing said. Not even a word. No exchanged glances. No presence acknowledged. Not a head nod. Not even a raised eyebrow. Nothing. Speechless. Expressionless. Just got up. And left. Mr. Guard's warm demeanor was starting to seem intimate by comparison. Another appeared drugged—glossy-eyed, spaced out; the remaining two seemed somewhat better.

I had prepared a number of subjects, anticipating the necessity for a monologue. But this slowly developed into a reasonable dialogue, nothing existential, just basic. And I quickly learned a secret. They needed company, attention. Simple talk, encouragement, not lecturing.

An hour passed. Eitan and the chaplain reappeared; we returned to the latter's office.

"How'd it go?"

"Okay."

"What did you talk about?"

"Nothing special. Just talked."

"Did you enjoy it?"

"Yeah. Sure," I said, befuddled.

Thus began my first day in prison.

My visceral circuitry had run an entire gamut, from piqued to frazzled, my nerves numbed from overload.

As far as the prison itself was concerned, nothing out of the ordinary had occurred, yet I felt giddy, disoriented, overwhelmed. But, simultaneously, I became infused with curiosity, energized, fascinated by this fast-paced, self-contained community, as if viewing, wide-eyed, a newly discovered country, an unplotted territory.

By the time I'd arrive home, I thought, things would resume normal proportions. When I settled in, I reasoned, prison would turn out to be just another workplace. No place could stay so richly intriguing, mesmerizing, for an extended period.

That was over thirteen years ago. And it has.

2

Nitzon Prison

Hertzel Aviton was raised in Tel Aviv, one of a dozen siblings in a family that was not well to do. He began stealing shoes, fruit, and bicycles at eleven years of age. In his teens he graduated to burglaries, embarking on multiple crime sprees. Photos show that he was a very slim, olive-skinned youth with jet black hair.

At age 21, he was apprehended shortly after a violent armed robbery of a local cafe. He did not cooperate during the police interrogation, defiantly holding his mouth full of water during the entire questioning. He and his accomplice, Urie Wolf, the son of a physician, landed five years in prison.

In December, 1978, Aviton, then aged 30, was released after completing his sentence. He briefly traveled abroad, accompanied by

Orly Arbiv, a woman who would herself become a convicted criminal and give birth to their son, the first child ever raised in an Israeli prison.

Ironically, that very month, the Israeli government was launching a brand new 700-inmate prison in Ramleh, a small city twenty minutes southeast of Tel Aviv, where I would serve as chaplain. Physically, it was identical to all the country's other maximum security prisons. Its agenda, though, was different: This prison would offer literacy classes, group therapy, and professionally supervised drug rehabilitation.

No one was more directly affected by crime and drugs than the prison service. Crime kept its buildings bursting from overpopulation. Drugs fueled the crime. Outside, in the school system and in the media, the department of education was stirring public awareness about a problem already recognized as rampant. Prisons were a battlefield and breeding ground for drug use and the drug trade; not for nothing have prisons been called institutes of higher learning for crime. Spearheading a fight against the prison drug industry would demand brains and guts.

Luckily, the right man was already there. Just a few years earlier, Roni Nitzon had completed his obligatory army stint. He stood around five feet eight inches, had a medium build, and light brown hair kept in a neat crew cut. Nitzon had first joined the prison staff as an education professional and counselor for troubled youth. "In society there are many groups willing to take care of the needy," he said in an interview. "It's hard to find people willing to do that with prisoners. It's simply not 'popular.' When you get to know them, though, you see they are human. They've been dealt a bad deal in life. I think I can help, and hope to try."

His sincerity caught the eyes of his superiors. In fact, years later, Nitzon's mother related to me how he'd take items from his own home to make life easier for the inmates in his prison. He was soon sent off to officer training and in December, 1978 acquiesced to becoming the new prison's first warden.

Nitzon did not fool himself: "I know we will be trying to

initiate something which will be fought by many of the prisoners. Crime and drugs involve a lot of power. It's going to be an uphill battle. But I believe in the cause. No one likes extortion, violence, or power struggles between warring gangs, which is what we have now. But, I believe we can help everyone get out of this mess. There are also many innocent prisoners who just want to finish their sentence and go home. We owe it to everyone to be successful. It's going to be tough. I believe we can do it."

The new prison would have everything standard in all other prisons when it came to manpower and security resources. It would also house hundreds of tough men from the overall prisoner populace. Its unique focus, however, would be a couple of special wards where those wishing to receive an education and undergo organized rehab could roam around freely all day, receive weekly family visits, exercise, watch TV, and have access to the library—and to a fighting chance for a normal life beyond prison.

The prison service knew it would have to tighten enforcement of the existing drug laws if the new model were to be successful. There are many ways drugs get into prisons anywhere. Commonly, they're concealed on the body when prisoners return from court appearances, for example. Expensive drug detectors are designed to catch some of that. For drugs not exposed by detectors, including those hidden inside the body, there are body searches.

No one likes body searches—particularly hardened

criminals, who often feel all they have is their personal pride. For them, body searches are experienced as an affront to any remaining human dignity. These body searches, and the intense loathing they inspired, would be evident in the explosive events to come.

Nitzon's first half year as warden was very successful. Official stats reported over forty drug busts of hashish, opium, cocaine, and heroine inside the prison. Drug use was down from seventy to only two percent. There was full attendance at classes, and drug rehab programs were progressing well. Participating inmates were beginning to show their appreciation. Most importantly, the atmosphere throughout the prison was clearly more relaxed and peaceful.

But Hertzel Aviton, too, was busy resuming his life as a crime kingpin outside the prison. It was May 2, 1979, a sunny Wednesday afternoon. The site was the north Tel Aviv branch of Bank Leumi, located on a quiet side street of a neighborhood full of academicians and professionals. The bank had just closed its doors for the day. Tellers were clearing off their countertops, tallying the money in their accounts.

A white four door Subaru quietly pulled up to the nearby sidewalk, unnoticed.

Suddenly, three masked and armed men, including one carrying a *submachine* gun, leapt out. They rushed the bank, spraying bullets as they ran. All surveillance cameras were destroyed instantly. The robbers shattered the front door and entered. Inside, the dozen workers needed no more convincing than the sharp order, "Everybody down, *now*, or we'll blow you away!"

Within minutes, the three had filled huge duffel bags with everything they could get their hands on: checks, cash, money orders, coins. Outside, an off-duty cop happening by pulled his gun and emptied a bullet into the chest of the waiting driver. The sound of the shooting confused the three men inside, who believed the police had arrived and had surrounded the building. The robbers panicked, screaming to one another, "Police. Let's get out!" They exited wildly, spraying bullets in all directions - even throwing *hand-grenades.* Outside, they pushed the unconscious driver out of the way and sped away with the goods.

Police commissioner Moses Tiyomkim immediately arrived at the scene and would soon announce on national television that, "In all my years with the force, I've never seen anything this wild. This is the beginning of a new period of crime in Israel."

Well, there are always sources of information when it comes to tracking down hard-core criminals. Besides, it's hard to hide in a country barely the size of New Jersey. That very night, five prime suspects were apprehended, including Urie Wolf, Hertzel Aviton, and Aaron (Hertzel's younger brother by five years).

The elder Aviton was incarcerated in Nitzon's prison during his trial, a trial that commanded the attention of the entire country and during which witnesses were too terrified to testify. Aviton's sister, Yafo, 28, called as state witness, disappeared, only to reappear at trial's end. Aviton's brother-in-law, Sam Shifroto, became hysterical and collapsed on the witness stand, his face ashen, his eyes bulging out, spit dripping from his lips. Medical and psychological examinations concluded these symptoms were authentic, and he was hospitalized. During one hearing, an alert guard investigated noise he heard in an overhead air duct, only to discover some of Aviton's cohorts on their way to free him.

With daily excursions to court, though under unprecedented security, it was feared Aviton was smuggling drugs back into the prison. He was not excluded from the zero-tolerance drug policy, so he was obliged to undergo body searches. This infuriated the man who was commonly considered the reigning king of the Israeli underworld. He vowed to kill Nitzon.

The first foreboding clouds of this vendetta began to appear just the following month, June 1979. A live hand grenade was found under the bedroom window of the child of the officer in charge of body searches. A week later, a death threat, addressed to "the administration" was found in the prison dining hall. "You will pay in blood," it warned. "You are not playing with children."

On Wednesday, July 11, a personal note - in the form of a hand-grenade, Israeli army series 12/74 - was sent to Warden Nitzon. It's pin had been pulled. "I woke up at 6:30 to get ready for work. I tried opening the door, but felt something stopping it. I was able to glance out and saw a package suspended—one end of a wire to the outside handle of the door, the other to the banister of the stairs. I knew it was a bomb. I thought I had detonated it. I turned around and leaped head first to the opposite wall, doubled up and waited for the explosion. When that didn't happen, I gathered my wife and young daughter and went out to the balcony to ask someone to call the police."

"Do you have second thoughts about your rehab efforts, now?" asked one of Israel's leading magazines the following day.

"Maybe at one point I did," Nitzon said with his usual thoughtfulness. "But, as time goes on, my conviction not to become intimidated just strengthens. I'd feel a terrible emptiness the rest of my life if I'd buckle now. We believe we're doing the best thing for everybody. You can't let some bad apples make you back off. I'm lucky I have a brave wife. She says she married me knowing there'd be dangers. I am, though, concerned for my little daughter. That bothers me."

On April 10, 1980, a supreme court decision limiting the scope and frequency of body searches was issued after three prisoners incarcerated in Nitzon's prison had appealed for an injunction. Signed by Mr. Aaron Barak, who would eventually rise to head the Supreme Court of Israel, the decision's main thrust was that the discipline necessary in prison does not negate an inmate's basic human rights or self-esteem and that the prison service must learn to cope with drug smuggling using more moderate means.

On May 8, 1980, the criminal court dished out to Aviton the maximum fifteen years for leading the banking robbery a year earlier. In ensuing years, details would trickle out showing that, from the moment Aviton entered prison, plans were under way for his escape. In interviews, his girlfriend Arbiv later claimed she had been pivotal in the execution of these plans.

In 1981, the prison service was told that Aviton's father was critically ill. A compassion-visit to his apartment was urgently requested. On Wednesday morning, September 23, 1981, Aviton was led, shackled hand and foot and surrounded by armed guards, to visit his ailing father in the latter's third story apartment in central Israel. After spending enough time with his father for the guards to have relaxed, Aviton was allowed to go to the bathroom. He somehow managed to release his cuffs, then slipped down a rope, readied for this purpose, on the side of the building. A waiting getaway car whisked him away.

The entire Israeli law enforcement network went on high alert. Aviton's hatred for them all was well known. His intentions to exact revenge for the system's perceived affronts to his dignity were common knowledge. A national search of unprecedented scope was immediately launched. While an escapee, Aviton gave a secret interview with one of Israel's national dailies. He claimed he was innocent and had no intention to harm anyone.

But for Warden Nitzon it was already too late. On Sunday, December 13, 1981 at exactly seven in the morning, as usual, Roni Nitzon left his home on Sharira Street, Rishon Lezion, in central Israel. After inspecting it for bombs, he entered his new white prison-service-issue Renault 4. He drove out of his driveway and headed down the main street. He got about two hundred yards, exactly opposite the Ofokim elementary school, and slowed down for the right turn that would take him out of the neighborhood. He'd been down this road a million times before.

He may not even have noticed the vehicle waiting for him at the corner, a blue van with engine running, two men waiting impatiently inside. Nitzon slowed down, put on his right turn blinker, and began the turn. That was the sign. Before he knew what was happening, the van shot out in front of him, blocking his path. A masked Hertzel Aviton jumped out, carrying an Uzie submachine gun that he shoved into Nitzon's face.

There were many eyewitnesses standing close by: adults on their way to work, children going to school. At that very moment,

Nitzon's own wife, Rachel, 32, was taking their five-year- old daughter to kindergarten. Before he had a chance to react or to draw his own pistol, Nitzon, still not recognizing the particular peril he was in, was able to beseech, "I'll give you whatever you want, my possessions, money, anything. Just leave me alone."

"What are you talking about?" Aviton screamed, "I've come to pay you back!" Opening fire, he emptied 22 bullets into Nitzon's head and upper torso. Nitzon's sunglasses flew out the window. Blood spurted in all directions. Warden Roni Nitzon died on the spot.

Over twenty years after Nitzon's death, I look around the very prison in which he served as its first warden and see an entirely different world than he did. These days, it's understood as a "given" that each ward has two or more dedicated social workers, as well as education officers, rabbis like me and those under me, drug rehab programs, counseling - anything prisoners could need to get back on the human track if they choose to do so. And I see a lot of smiles and a lot of hope on a lot of faces.

Yearly, I do the memorial service at the Tel Aviv military cemetery in Roni Nitzon's honor. Afterwards, my wife, Miriam, and I share coffee with Nitzon's elderly parents at their home. And sitting there, sipping coffee with them and remembering their son, reinforces for me, despite an understandable sorrow, some things I've always felt: That each and every one of us has the capability to change the world around us for the better—that part of the world which is ours to change. Sometimes the price is high. But, in the end, the good always wins.

3

The Assistant Who Got Canned

I was just warming up to my new job when I found an assistant. Rather, he found me. "I see you're new here," he said. "I might be able to help." It was then and there that I learned that my position had a budget for employing a prisoner as a helper, a welcome discovery because the responsibilities at this large bustling—700 inmate—maximum-security prison had to be digested systematically.

Joseph, 25, medium-built, brown hair, dark-skinned, had been working satisfactorily on the cleaning detail, but was looking for a small change. Smiley, congenial, he'd be easy to get along with.

He had not yet been tried for the multiple armed robberies and sexual offenses of which he was accused.

My hunch that he'd be helpful proved correct. Joseph assisted with the tons of bureaucratic paperwork: reporting student attendance (prisoners receive a monthly stipend for study), recording distribution of holiday supplies, and paying teachers' salaries. Additionally, he ran errands in the vast expanses of our building and acted as liaison between inmates and administration.

During our first few months, he tried explaining to me the intricacies of his case. Aware it was high-profile, I avoided listening, though I heard it anyway through conversations with other prisoners and from the media. He unequivocally claimed innocence. Did he have a choice? The question of his guilt will always puzzle me.

A productive year passed quickly. We increased enrollment in our study program, and initiated a number of others which were well-received. All in all we kept things rolling.

One morning, seated in my office, I noticed a sharp decline, a crack in his mood. His natural optimism had soured.

"I can't take it anymore," he sighed, his shoulders heaving as if he were about to burst out crying.

Odd, I thought, *that's out of the blue.* "What?" I asked.

"Being taken to court," he said.

I was listening.

Joseph sat, slumped forward, his forehead held by his upturned open right palm. His pained tone said it all. "We leave prison at 6:00 A.M., stuffed shoulder-to-shoulder like sardines in a service bus, travel three long hours handcuffed to the guy next to us on a cushionless seat. Then we get dropped off at the district central courthouse down south."

"So?" I asked. His unusual mood intrigued me. After all, this was an upbeat guy.

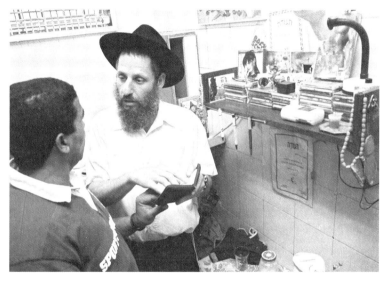

"They cram us into a four-by-four-yard windowless basement waiting room. No heating, *no* ventilation." His face contorted just relating it. "I don't even smoke cigarettes. But the others, chain-smoke everything—cigarettes—dope. You name it. The air is so putrid I feel dizzy, nauseous. You know what it's like, sitting there, unable to breathe, for six hours, until they take us out to our hearings upstairs, in the courtroom?"

During a year and a half working together, I'd never seen him so much as complain. This must have been boiling up slowly.

I investigated, partly out of employer concern. During one hearing, I learned from the escorting guards, Joseph broke down weeping like a baby, begging to be freed from this weekly torture.

"Is that true?" I asked him.

"Yes," he admitted sheepishly, embarrassed that his weakness had become the talk of the prison. What happened was this. The judge had ordered that Joseph be brought directly to his mid-day hearings, not from the early morning with the other prisoners. This was a humanitarian gesture, to spare him from the waiting-cell ordeal. The harried police escorts, brimming with pressing responsibilities had disregarded that order.

Joseph lost faith in the judge's ability to withstand pressure. "Look," he leveled with me, "I'll tell you what's really eating me. Part of the charges are for sexual offenses. There are a number of women's rights groups pressuring the court to fry me. If the judge can't enforce a simple order, a basic consideration like this, should I believe he'll be able to stand up against all those demands?"

The judge, I thought, *wasn't the one who* put *you here.*

Anxiety for his trial's outcome was ruining his cool. I saw it in his edgy stance, nervous movement, the fear deep in his eyes.

The day of the verdict, I happened to have worked late. When I entered Joseph's ward that evening, he had still not returned from court. I waited for what seemed an eternity. On such days, the entire ward is tense, the air thick, as if eighty men are holding their breath simultaneously. It's as if one man's destiny could act as an omen—good or bad—for all. To me, the clearest indication that Joseph's verdict was on everyone's mind was that *no one* talked about it.

Finally, at 7:30, Joseph entered, a horrified look on his face, his wide eyes bulging out. Shuffling by, without even acknowledging my presence, he immediately got into an argument with another prisoner in his cell.

Joseph: "What are you doing here?"

Nisim: "The ward's officer put me in."

Joseph: "Why?"

Nisim gave his reason, to which Joseph—still obviously dazed—barked, "Just don't smoke here. The smoke rises to the ceiling, then comes down on me in my bed," he said, pointing to his top bunk bed. "My mother gets mad. She says the smell of tobacco doesn't come out in the wash. She says I smell." Joseph, a nonsmoker, then threatened, "I'll throw you out if you smoke!"

The tension thus cracked, conversation reverted to the subject on everyone's mind.

Nisim: "What happened?"

Joseph: "The judge found me guilty on all four counts."

Nisim: "Four?"

Joseph: "Yeah. He had no clue what was coming off! I actually corrected him when he announced, 'Guilty on *all* four counts'—there were *six* and one attempted break in. He didn't mention the other offenses."

Nisim: "Whoa! You're gonna sit for eight to ten."

Joseph: "Yeah. He found me innocent of stealing the gun. The bum. I was sure he'd find me guilty on that, but thought he'd at least let me off some of the other counts."

"How do you feel?" I interjected.

Joseph slowly shook his head. "I don't know... it's...," he stopped to think, sat down on the bottom bed, back bent, slumped forward. "It'll take time to digest. I'm 27, now, and won't get out 'till..." his voice trailed off, and almost inaudibly continued. "...Eight to ten years is a long time." He looked down at the ground. "What am I going to do then?"

This conversation represented the first time I ever heard Joseph refer to any of the charges against him in the first person. He was finally internalizing his situation. He used to say: "One charge is 'Illegal Possession of Firearms,'" or 'Intimidation with a Deadly Weapon.'" Now he said, "They claim *I* stole the gun," or "*I* shot it when I threatened her."

The cell fell silent. What could be said? Then Joseph's real anger exploded, "I kept telling my family the lawyer wasn't doing his job!" he yelled, banging his fist into his mattress. Inmates often believe the attorney is to blame, is only interested in the details of his *fees*, not of their cases.

Another common and bitter complaint is unexpected mid-case fee-hikes. In Joseph's case, this fell on him *three* times. The worst, right before the trial's end, he got hit up for an additional thirty thousand dollars. Rubbing salt in the wound, his attorney soon after bought a new Mercedes, infuriating Joseph's family, who was picking up the tab for legal fees. What choice did they have?

Later that evening, out in the kitchen, I asked one of the cooks, a prisoner, his opinion of Joseph's innocence or guilt.

"Of course he's guilty. It's hard to believe 'cause he's such a nice kid. He must be sick or something, like me. I'm a kleptomaniac, can't stop myself from stealing. I see something I like and I gotta take it. He must be sick."

"Think he'll ever admit to it?" "Never," he said laughing. "Forget it. Things like this a prisoner can never admit. Even after sentencing. Even after the appeal. That's just the way it goes."

Three weeks passed, work went as usual. A prisoner came running up to me, in the corridor, eyes wide with amazement, "Guess how long he got!" Still huffing, he blurted out, "Twenty-one years!"

What?—I thought—*that's* a number that never came up before.

That night, working late, I met Joseph upon his return from court. He had quickly deteriorated. He was a walking mummy. That number destroyed whatever was left of him.

"I can't believe it," he whispered. "There goes my life. A guy across the corridor who murdered his own nephew got off with 10. It's all public pressure. Judges are coming down hard on cases involving sexual offenses."

This was a talk from the heart, it had built up for over two years. There was more unsaid than said.

"Where's the proportions...?" He stopped, took a deep breath. "What about Miki who killed her own husband and got seven, reduced to five because of public pressure?" he whined. "Just my luck, cases like mine got a lot of publicity this week. The judge got nervous. I can't believe it, *twenty-one* years!"

Joseph stopped his monologue, but I knew the next line. All inmates utter it at this point.

"We're gonna appeal. The Supreme Court will have to reduce," they hope, but it means nothing. "I can't believe it! I'm twenty-seven. When I finally get outta here, I'll be near fifty!"

"Take it easy. Who came to court to hear the sentencing?"

"Just my brother."

"What did your lawyer say?"

"He said prosecution had wanted to make a deal if I'd admit guilt, but it would be against *his* conscience for *me* to admit to something I didn't do."

"What did prosecution say?"

"They only asked for thirteen."

The next day, my warden called me into his office explaining that Joseph wouldn't be allowed out of his ward anymore, except in my company. He'd been classified as a high-risk potential escapee. "All movement must be accompanied by you or another guard," he said. "By the way, we're watching closely for suicide."

The following week, Joseph moped all day, morning to night, stopped conversing with the other prisoners, and left his cell just to get food. His only remaining hope was an appeal to the Supreme Court, begging for mercy, requesting a sentence reduction. What leverage did he have working for him?

He could admit guilt. This would be anticlimactic after two years of claiming innocence. However, in Israel, the law is that after serving a quarter of their sentence, prisoners begin monthly prison leaves. In Joseph's case this could be in only five years. The big catch is, convicted sexual offenders *must* admit to guilt first! He would eventually have to admit, anyway.

The once self-assured, easygoing assistant, was now reduced to an empty broken shell. He'd soon be transferred away from the prison where he spent the first two years of incarceration. His decision to appeal—beg for reduction, admit guilt—were all long shots. He knew it. Overnight becoming an outcast—due to the nature of some of the crimes he was convicted of—Joseph would soon be very alone. I had no idea what he was going to do.

Whatever he did the assistant would be doing it alone.

4

Shmulik

It is 9:30 A.M. in the central corridor of the prison. Guards are running in my direction, an "emergency" look is plastered on their faces. Seven pass me, ordering, "Come!" Five more join them carrying clubs and gas masks.

We arrive at Ward C, the most vacuous ward in our institution. In it, every two prisoners share a 6' by 9' concrete cell which, despite yearly paint jobs, always looks like it is ready for the next. The ceramic tiles in the bathrooms are faded, the floor needs a good polishing.

The tension in the air is as thick as it gets. You feel it the moment you walk in.

Ward C houses problematic prisoners, restricted from contact with others. For example, a prisoner who spent an entire year stalking, then killing, the terrorist who ambushed and murdered his army officer brother was forbidden to mingle with the regular populace for fear of a revenge attack from Arab prisoners. Others are there due to personal feuds or mental problems.

The guards swung open the heavy metal doors leading into the ward. Thick, putrid black smoke hit us in the face. We forced ourselves to enter.

Tongues of flame shot out violently from the door of cell #12, reaching three or four feet over the top of the lintel. Three guards stood outside the cell door, frozen by the sight of the flames. Inside was a man.

The maintenance officer came rushing in. Taking in the situation he ordered, "Bring the water hose!"

Someone grabbed it and began running, but the thick black hose, wrapped around a circular holder on the wall, got within ten feet of the cell, knotted, and stopped.

Then came the improvisations. Two guards with a small pail ran back and forth from the nozzle to the cell, each run throwing his futile gallon of water on the huge flames. The plastic and Styrofoam mattress, blankets, and wooden table blazed on.

I turned to one of the guards familiar with the personalities in that ward, "Was the fire intentional?" Not thinking twice, he said, "Of course!"

There was hysterical crying from all sides—the guards

because they didn't know what to do, the prisoners thinking they were going to suffocate in their locked cells.

Considering the small size of the cell, I reasoned, the prisoner must have been roasted.

The guards started calling into the cell, "Shmulik jump, Shmulik jump out!"

I couldn't imagine any "Shmulik," unless an experienced stunt man bypassing those flames, which completely covered the entire door opening, fiercely spreading two feet beyond with intense crackling.

Then, turning around, I couldn't believe my eyes. Shmulik lay on the floor of the corridor. He had jumped! And lay there unconscious!

A medic ordered Shmulik removed from the corridor. Good idea. But, what about the other 80 prisoners and 20 guards choking to death?

Ultimately, the maintenance officer came up with a good idea. He walked down the hall and took the *fire extinguisher* off the wall. The fire extinguisher did its job in less than five minutes. The coughing, sputtering prisoners were taken out to the yard for air.

Outside the ward in the main hall Shmulik lay spread out, unconscious, shaking uncontrollably, until whisked away to the infirmary.

I asked one of the guards why Shmulik set fire to his room

like that; he could easily have been killed. "For attention. He wasn't getting what he wanted."

These situations are not uncommon in prisons. Some prisoner with nothing to lose cuts his wrist, stabs someone. Two minutes later he's got a "I didn't do anything look" of innocence on his face—in fifteen minutes he's forgotten all about it.

I returned to my office to do some paperwork.

Later that day, around 3:30 p.m., I had some work to do in Ward C. I went in to see how things were going. The prisoners were back to their normal routines. So were the guards. Cell #12 was also back to normal and repopulated. Shmulik was back.

5

What Would You Say?

One of the most difficult situations I face is when Jewish prisoners with heart-wrenching, pitiful childhoods and life-stories have committed sickening crimes and ask me, as their rabbi, if G-d will forgive them.

There is an abundance of social workers in the Israeli Prison Service—often two or more for every ward. Additionally, the prisoner can find a sympathetic ear in the officer in charge of the ward. However, neither of them evoke the natural confidence that prisoners have in the chaplain. Coming largely from Middle Eastern Oriental religious homes, religion is something respected and holy in their minds. Our job as rabbis is to be there for them. We are viewed as being close to the Almighty and having the answers. To us, they can open their hearts and minds. And they do.

"I never met my mother," Joel said, matter-of-factly. "I never met my real brothers and sisters, either. We moved here from France. My father was a building contractor. He built half of Holon [central Israel]. But after my birth he divorced my mother - or she left, he never really told me which.

"While I was still young, he remarried and had some kids. But then, he had a brain clot, became paralyzed, and we became desperately poor. I had to take to the streets to look for food. I scrounged through garbage to find it."

Joel's bright, shining eyes and warm smile made the conversation effortless. At 23, he was still young. His being in a special ward and prohibited from mingling with other prisoners gave me a vaguely uncomfortable feeling.

"My father, incapacitated from his condition, couldn't sustain even a minimal home. I had to sleep in cardboard boxes under the sky, in parks, in the street.

"I never stole stuff or anything like that. Over the years, I sold little things I came across. I did odd jobs and began to work in a factory during the day; at night I made money doing other things.

"Eventually I got married and we had a daughter. But my wife had a car accident and became paralyzed. The social worker assigned to us, because of our poor economic state, classified my wife and I as incapable of taking care of our daughter. We had no family to turn to for assistance, so the social welfare people decided to take her from us. Boom! Just like that.

"Crazy. I was trying my best to make some money, feed my wife and young child—boom!—I'm forced into battling against the whole system—just to keep my own daughter! Everyone knows you can't fight the government. They told me, 'Go to this office to file papers,' then they'd say, 'Go to that one for a signature,' back and forth. I couldn't keep working and fighting the system, too. The only thing I have in this world is my wife and daughter."

I sensed his approaching an unpleasant punch line. This is how prisoners build up justifications, "explaining" their past history, *then* telling you what they did.

My stomach started to churn.

"Yes, never having met my real mother, brothers, or sisters and being thrown to the streets for my survival at a young age, the only things I really have in life are my disabled wife and daughter, who the social worker decided to take away from us."

"Okay, so what did you do? I mean why are you here?" I finally asked.

"Well, when I saw that I was being sent aimlessly from one government office to the next with the social worker deciding to give my daughter to a foster family, I killed her."

"*What?*"

He *detailed* the murder of the social worker, which included hanging and subsequent dismemberment.

As he continued, I felt like I was in the front car of the largest roller coaster in America. I felt disgusted, amazed, nauseous, and speechless all at once.

"What did you *gain?* I mean, doing something like that wasn't going to get your daughter back."

"I don't know. I heard from other people in the city that the old buzzard took a lot of kids from their parents. Everyone told me it was a good thing I did to get rid of her. Besides, she deserved it; all I have in this world is my wife and daughter."

After diverting my thoughts to more pleasant things, like the beach and memories of skiing in Vermont, allowing my stomach to resume its normal composure, I finally gained enough presence to continue the conversation.

"Now, what do you want?"

"Well, my wife is thinking of a divorce. I haven't been sentenced yet. She told me she still loves me and doesn't really want a divorce. But if I get a life sentence, she wants a divorce."

"I think that sounds reasonable," I said, as images of the old social worker hanging from the ceiling flashed in my mind.

"My wife is all I have to live for. Without my daughter or my wife and no family to visit me, what do I have to live for? I'll just kill myself here."

I knew he was serious. (During the week following this conversation he attempted suicide twice.)

"Now, rabbi, you've heard my whole story. Tell me..."

At this point, he's dead serious. I know I'll be hard pushed to compose a response for the next question. I've heard it before, can feel when it's coming, and know I have no answer.

"What can I do to get G-d to forgive me?"

6

What's Your Name?

Life in prison is rough; as a staff member, you have to know how to get your way with the prisoners. You must know how to talk to them. I've figured it out. It's based on fear. Quiet, subliminal fear. That's what they respond to.

No, not the fear caused by yelling or threatening—that wouldn't work for any staffer, particularly one in my position. It would be demeaning, counterproductive.

So, when it comes to toughened criminals, no one is jailed for jay-walking—our clientele includes armed robbers, murderers—raising your voice isn't fitting. But how *do* you avoid being trampled?

The answer lies in two parts: one, adopting a solemn, emotionless, facial-expression; two, quietly uttering, "What's your name?"

These three words, uttered in a cold monotone, translate in the prisoner's mind as "I'm reporting you higher up" without really having to say it.

Stating explicitly, "I'm going to report you," would be falling into a trap. You'd be *re*acting, wasting negative emotion; you'd be caught momentarily off-balance. Worse, threats evoke a verbal exchange from which inmates frequently emerge victorious, winning because *they* are experts in psychology, body language, and deftly and spontaneously creating ingenious mercy-evoking tactics.

Nothing surpasses this hard-learned lesson. No outright threats, no confrontation. Three magic words, recited impassionately with the quiet authority of someone who reports daily to the security officer and the warden—the warning is implied. It works, because in the recipient's mind it conjures up a written report with unknown contents, unforeseeable implications, by an officer, whose impersonal demeanor shows he'll win when *you're* finally brought to a disciplinary hearing. But, more damaging, it'll go into *your* personal files. *That's* forever.

Life in the slammer means an eternal undercurrent of psychological power struggles between staff and inmates. A prisoner standing in the corridor, idly conversing with a buddy, ostensibly innocuous, can be viewed through experienced eyes as a plan being hatched. The prisoner's not supposed to be hanging around for no reason. For you, this is a minor headache, for him, an exercise in manipulation. Prisoners test and attempt to control staff constantly.

Sammy was someone I didn't want hanging around our program's classroom unsupervised. He was a graduate of too many army commando units, too strong—220 pounds—and just a bit too "helpful."

He voluntarily washed the floors and windows after morning studies at 11:00 and cleaned the toilet—assignments very hard to get volunteers for. He remained alone there during the 12:00 p.m. security roll-call instead of being in his ward. His hanging around *without* my directives, I didn't like.

He was uncontrollable. Here's a sample conversation.

Me: "Sammy, I want you to go back to the ward after class."

Sammy: "Okay. But first I have to clean the floors. Look how dirty they are."

In the meantime he's thrown water and detergent on half the floor and commenced mopping. You'll look pretty stupid leaving that mess all over the floor stopping him now. You lose.

A couple of days later, he's with a cellmate, one you *do* allow to remain after morning studies. They're both washing the floors. "Sammy, I don't want you hanging around, doing the floor, without my telling you to."

Sammy: "Why? Look how dirty it is, and what's the difference between the classroom and the dining hall? There, inmates clean and work without supervision. Besides, I'm here with Abe."

Me: "The security officer forbids inmates to be *here* unsupervised, even doing the floors."

Sammy: "Okay. Just let me just finish the floors, then I'll go back to the ward."

In the course of this dialogue, all the chairs get overturned onto the tables, and there's no time to look for someone else to help. You lose.

Sunday morning arrives. The shelves have been washed, the coffee corner has been neatly rearranged, the room is spiffy.

Everything you've been meaning to get around to doing is done. Morning studies are over. Here comes Sammy, with the officer-in-charge of his ward.

Sammy says to me, "The officer said I can finish cleaning and be tallied while in the classroom." And, turning to the commander of his ward, *your* superior, for confirmation, asks, "Right?"

Then in a voice loud enough for both the officer and you to hear, "Isn't the class looking nice today? I got all those shelves organized."

You lose.

That's it. You've had it! It's going to be put to an end.

There's nothing wrong per se with what he's doing. It's just bad policy letting an inmate call the shots.

The following day, *immediately* after the morning studies, I call Sammy aside and quietly, almost whispering, say, "Sammy, make sure you're back in the ward. Now!"

He jumps into, "Why," and "How come," all kinds of arguments and manipulations. I imagine that placing the chairs on the tables has already entered his mind. But my composure and unswerving glare fix him motionless.

He finishes his semi-threats and half-begging mannerisms. Then, almost inaudibly, I mutter the mystical phrase: "What's your name?"

Of course, I know.

He registers, is just about to counter, when I throw the knockout line, cleanly delivered, but effective. I intentionally, delicately whisper, forcing his face to be drawn two inches from mine, just close enough: "What's your *full* name?"

Sammy goes cold, the blood drains from his face. "Leave... me alone," he stammers. "I... don't... wanna... mess... with... you," he gets out, backing off down the hall, heading up the steps back to his ward.

I'm left standing all by myself, smiling.

You just have to know how to talk to people.

7

You Gotta Be Kidding

A fellow in one of our drug rehabilitation programs had a business renting cheap automobiles to insurance companies as replacements for policy holders' stolen cars. He thereafter stole the replacement car from the policy owner using his duplicate keys, *and* submitted a theft claim to *his* insurance company reporting the "theft." Of course, during the interim his company continued to bill for rental.

But that wasn't the reason he sat in jail. He'd also robbed five banks.

"I once went into a big supermarket and decided to make some good money. So, I went down an empty aisle with the cart, collecting things from this shelf and from that one. I was just acting normally, doing my shopping. Making sure no one was watching, I pushed the cart into a shelf, knocking over a bottle of oil which dropped, broke, and spilled all over the floor. I made another round until there were other customers nearby, then intentionally slipped on the oil, of course making real sure everyone got a full view. Next, I went through the whole injured act. I was beautiful, if I may say so. They called the store manager. Naturally, I kept the performance going until escorted into the manager's office.

"They wanted me to sign some papers saying I wasn't hurt. The more they pressed me to sign, the more I said it hurt. Every time they'd mention the papers—oh boy, did it hurt! 'How 'bout some money?' they asked. When the price finally passed a grand, the pain decreased until it got just right, at which point the pain let up enough for me to sign, take the dough and split outta there. The most important thing was to make sure there were enough customers milling around who saw me fall.

"I have a buddy to whom I divulged this technique. I told him he could make all kinds of money. I told him to go into a very large supermarket and make sure he made lots of noise. He should do the same as me, except when he falls he should go down with a large bang, make lots of noise, the more the better, as if he just fell out of a moving car. He shouldn't get up until the ambulance arrives, then get admitted to the hospital for a few days complaining of head pains. Afterwards, he should get released and come back complaining about dizziness, unable to do simple things, like read a paper, cook, or drive. He should be especially careful if he needed to drive because the insurance companies would likely send investigators to check his story out. If he got caught, he could just say he has off days, and on days—that was an "on" one. To make a long story short, it's over five years and he's still collecting $2,700 every month. They want to settle with him for $200,000, but it's not worth it. I told him when he's ready he should move away.

"Another time, I got picked up for speeding. When I took out my driver's license, which was forged anyway, the traffic cops saw my gun. They said, 'Get out slowly,' and made me put my hands on the car. They asked me for a license for the gun. I said I didn't have one. They took the gun, ordering me to follow them to the station. When we arrived, they asked me all kinds of questions, but I refused to answer, saying I wanted to make a phone call. I called my wife and said I was in the police station 'cause I found a gun and was on my way to the police station to turn it in when I got stopped for speeding. They wanted me to sign all kinds of papers, but I refused. They said I have to. I said I wouldn't, and, if they insisted, I'd take the gun, go back, put it where I found it, and they could find it themselves. I'd even tell them where I put it. They finally let me go, but threatened that if any crimes were found to be committed with the gun, they'd come after me. I told them there were never any crimes committed with it. They asked how would I know. I told them I can just smell it on the gun.

"Another time, I was with my mother-in-law at her house and there was a crack in the wall. The carpenter said he wanted six or seven thousand dollars to fix it. I told her I could get it fixed for nothing, and in fact get her paid for it to be fixed. The only condition was she'd have to keep her mouth shut. At first she didn't want to agree, then when she saw I didn't care, said OK. I told her to leave the house and then went out and drove the jeep into the living room, through the wall. The insurance company came and gave her 10 days in a great hotel and fixed the house. The car insurance fixed the car.

"Another time, I bought a car for $1,800 and it started to make noise as if it had been shot. So I put a large pillow between me and the steering wheel, put on the safety belt, and drove it into a wall. When I reported it to the insurance company, they paid the whole price. In addition, I made them pay for all the repairs and parts put into the car. I had slips of repairs and parts from other cars—they paid for it all."

"Another time, I ran into a guy's car. He burst out yelling at me, so I got out and hit him. He started to curse and threaten me. I refused to give him my social-security and phone numbers, so he wrote down the plate's number. When we got to court, his lawyer bugged me 'cause he talked too much. I got up and said, 'I have something to say, and he should shut up because he is talking too much. The story is that I got out and the guy didn't want to give me *his* number and tried to hit me. So I hit him.' The guy yelled and carried on that it was a lie. But I insisted. 'Anyway,' I said to the lawyer, 'if someone tried to hit you, wouldn't you hit him back?' The lawyer said he didn't think so. So I said, 'You're not sure—maybe yes and maybe no. Well, I am.' Anyhow, the judge fined me 150 bucks. Believe me, if I could hit the guy again for a 150 bucks, it would be worth it. Really. I'm not kidding."

8

You Can't Jump to Conclusions

A logistical decision had been made to move ward A's inmates to ward D and vise versa. Exchange day had arrived.

Regulations demand large numbers of guards to supervise that such events pass in an orderly manner. The prisoners, carrying their mattresses and personal belongings, did, indeed, move quietly and obediently. Things were going well, with a feeling of cooperation between inmates and staff prevailing.

Suddenly, we heard shouting, a large commotion, in one of the wards up ahead. Six guards, myself included, took off in that direction.

We entered the ward. There, in the middle of the central corridor, separating two rows of cells, stood the officer in charge with three other officers. They were in front of the door of the cell that was the source of the noise.

Inside this cell was an inmate pacing around impatiently, wildly waving a thick wooden table leg. Out of his incoherent hysterical screams, all I could decipher were isolated phrases, "I'll show...," "Why can't...," which I took for complaints, threats—or both. His clothes, facial expressions, and body language were those of a repeat offender—no stranger to prison. He looked drugged: jerky motions, unnatural tilt to his head.

This uncontrolled screaming continued for over 20 minutes. At one point, he violently threw the rest of the table, some plates, cups, and a radio at the heavy metal cell door, then continued banging on the walls and door with the table leg.

The officer in charge tried cooling him down. "Just tell me what you want," I imagined him asking, though I stood barely out of hearing range. The inmate momentarily ceased screaming, relaxed, and answered. Apparently, he was expressing his desires or demands. Then, as if answering an invisible psychic signal, he flipped out—flailing, madly circling his small living space, throwing things at the door, banging the walls and door with the table leg.

Next, the process repeated itself. They spoke, the prisoner acquiesced to some conditions, inaudible to me; then, when it looked like the end, he flipped out again, entering another crazed tantrum.

I cautiously approached, and looked into the cell, "What's the problem?"

"I don't want to be moved to another ward," he answered.

"Why?"

On the verge of answering, he zonked out, gazing off into space as if trying to remember something.

Ten tense minutes passed. The prisoner, apparently settled, agreed to speak with the officer in charge inside his cell. I assumed a resolution was near.

The inmate laid down his table leg weapon. The guards warily opened the cell door, the officer entered. The officer took him aside; they spoke quietly. It looked as if the inmate had received satisfactory promises and that he'd come out of his own volition.

Then, with no warning, the prisoner began ramming his head against the concrete wall. Not like a kindergarten kid getting attention, rather throwing his entire body, bashing his head with all his might. His skull split open, blood poured over his sideburns, down his face.

"Get some men in here!" the officer yelled. "This guy's gonna hurt himself."

Five burly guards burst into the narrow cell and tried, unsuccessfully, to wrench the bloody inmate out into the corridor. There was insufficient room to maneuver. The struggle accelerated.

Eventually, exerting enormous effort, the guards wrestled him out, though he continued battling with all his might.

"Cuff 'im!" commanded the officer, which took *seven* guards, all the while the inmate violently flailing his arms and kicking like a rodeo bull. Eventually, his arms secured behind his back, it took these same guards to get his legs under control.

"Get him to the infirmary!" the officer directed. All the while the inmate incessantly kicked and yelled.

I escorted this weird entourage to the end of the corridor, then stopped in deep thought. The insanity of the past hour hit me. I had personally witnessed this entire scene, beginning to end.

Let's say someone *else* happened to be observing outside in the corridor. All he saw was: an inmate yelling, throwing things in his cell, discussions, five guards bursting in, a violent scuffle, a bleeding inmate dragged out into the corridor, seven guards handcuffing him against his will, dragging him away.

The logical conclusion someone reasonable would arrive at would be that the scuffle and his wounds resulted from unnecessary force.

Who would imagine the head injuries self-inflicted, the initial scuffle to prevent additional damage, with the guards now taking him to the infirmary for patching up?

Now you've heard a true story which changed the way *I*

think about things of which I may have had an opinion but hadn't actually witnessed.

You really can't jump to conclusions.

9

Adolph Eichmann

For years, I felt a deep unease each day upon entering my Ramleh Prison office. Just two stories, fifteen yards directly above my head, Adolph Eichmann had been executed. The final detail of his May 31, 1962 hanging haunted me, even though I'd been a child still living in New York when it happened.

It happened in an exclusive one-man mini-ward and execution room, home for the last two years of Eichmann's life, especially erected on the roof of the prison building.

Even approaching death, Eichmann was calculating—a Nazi characteristic. His final moments were planned, rehearsed. He read prepared statements expressing gratitude to the German Fatherland and to Argentina, his place of refuge.

Then as his last request, he made a final toast, finishing a bottle of wine.

While being led to the gallows, he refused an offer for a blindfold, sneering, "I don't need it."

The noose was placed around his neck. His body dropped through the opened trap door. He swayed back and forth. Justice, finally, had been meted out. The room fell silent.

Then, breaking the quietude, Eichmann's wine-primed bladder released onto the roof of our building.

Pouring, then slowing. *Drip. Drip. Drip.*

I wondered: Didn't history's greatest expert on mortality know a dead man's full bladder releases? Wasn't this a concluding gesture of contempt toward victims turned vindicators? A last vengeful shot at the people he so desperately struggled to wipe from the earth? For years, my tormented mind's ear recorded the dripping above my head.

Drip. Drip. Drip.

Although born ten years after the Holocaust, I, like so many others, feel its traumatizing effect through the people closest to my world.

My wife Miriam's father and mother lost both sets of parents, a combined total of eight siblings, and a daughter. After watching Nazi strongmen snatch her father off the street, my mother-in-law was taken to Auschwitz (1.25 million killed). There, she stood with her mother and two brothers. Mordechai 5, David *4 days old*, in the selection line: healthy, to the right; feeble, young, old, unfit for work, left—to the gas-chambers. A nameless woman tapping her on the back, whispered, "If you want *any* of your family to survive, give Mordechai to your mother." She did, never seeing any of the three again. She has suffered agonizing, guilt-ridden, sleepless nights ever since. She saved a pair of German army boots, found on the death march, for her father who she knew would be shoeless. She hoped against hope to find him. She never did.

Uncle Simon, too, lost both parents; he and Bertha were married *in* Auschwitz. Now in their 80s, they are still childless, due to Dr. Mengele's medical experiments. Uncle Meir, survived, too. He and his two-year-old cousin were both entrusted by their parents to local farm women for concealment. Prepayment for Meir's upkeep held out; his cousin's did not, and he ended up strangled and buried in a field.

In sentences that drift off, averted glances, cynicism, and the inability to feel simple human pleasures, the pain quietly permeates our lives. Still at one time, I'd thought years of work's daily routine had drowned out Eichmann's memory.

One day in late 1998, the phantom dripping returned.

Adolph's sons, Deiter and Professor Ricardo Eichmann, publicly requested that the Israeli National Archives release to them their father's 1,200 page diary. Handwritten during the period awaiting his verdict, it had been preserved, unexposed to public scrutiny, despite periodic researcher requests.

Predictably, this elicited an international outpouring of pressure, a cacophony of self-righteous debate around—of all things—inheritance rights!

Resolution of the matter in international-public-image-conscious Israel would float between the Prime Minister's legal advisor and the Attorney General.

The blatant *chutzpah* of the case left much of Israel dumbstruck, especially death-camp survivors and their offspring. The request, portrayed as a humanitarian/legal issue, rubbed stinging salt into the still agonizingly deep wounds of a nation attempting to return to itself.

The thought of his sons receiving the memoirs was chilling.

First, the audacity! Their father murdered *millions*—men, women, and children—in cold blood. Would his sons, commanding any price from publishing companies, reap financial gain? I imagined the papers stained with blood. Eichmann himself seemed to have conceived their publication, *specifically* requesting "ten copies for my wife, one for me."

Worse, German commentators, journalists and historians were dying to get *first* shot at them, chomping at the bit to revive the "I was a follower, not issuer of orders" motif. Exoneration (not to mention revenge) was widely considered the author's primary ulterior motive for writing.

Son Deiter declared openly, "Israel is playing games with my father's diaries, for decades not delivering what is coming to us, our father's final words. *His* explanations of the truth; his life's story. I demand the original copy, I demand that they don't publicize *any* part of it."

Elie Weisel retorted, "Maybe he saw in these writings an answer to his judges, maybe even a *revenge* against the Jews who dared sentence him to death."

What transpired with Eichmann from the allied forces' victory until his demise?

After the war ended, in 1945, Eichmann was captured by U.S. troops, but escaped before they knew who they had. He then lived as an anonymous lumberjack for a couple of years in a Northern German village, careful not to contact his wife and kids.

Around 1950, allegedly with the help of a Fransiscan priest in Genoa, Italy and the Nazi underground organization ODESSA, Eichmann secured a refugee passport under the name Richard Klement from the Displaced Persons Relief Center in the Vatican. In mid-July he sailed to Argentina, being joined two years later by his wife and three children.

Eichmann, now Ricardo Clamant, had a new life down in Buenos Aires, 7,380 air-miles from Berlin. Together with other trusted SS fugitives, they became a tight-knit community. Eichmann tried rabbit farming and a laundry operation but failed, finally settling for a job as a foreman in a Mercedes-Benz factory in the Buenos Aries suburb of Suarez.

Quiet life, new identity—even the local Jews didn't know who the new neighbor was.

During the early evening hours of May 11, 1960, 54-year-old Ricardo was returning from work to his home on Grivaldi Street in a suburb of Buenos Aries. Two parked cars waited on the corner. Upon his approach, one flashed its high beams, blinding him. Instantaneously, two men jumped out, shoving him into the second car within seconds. Blindfolded, hand and footcuffed, adorned with sunglasses, he was covered with a blanket on the back floor. A 45-minute drive took them to a waiting rented apartment.

"What is your name?"

Alert, as always, sensing the futility of denying what his capturers already knew, he conceded, "Eichmann. My name is Adolph Eichmann."

But the wiliest fugitive ever was already looking to curry favor in his Mossad captors' eyes. "I know Hebrew," he said, proving it by reciting—In the beginning G-d created the heaven and earth—in its original language.

He smiled, a smirk, wicked beyond comprehension. A

diabolical flash flickered, ever so quickly, in his eyes. "I know more," he offered.

Then, totally shocking everyone present, he repeated the single most treasured line in the Jewish tradition, the last words to leave the dying lips of millions of *his* own victims, men, women, children. "Hear O Israel, the L-rd our G-d, the L-rd is One."

The courtroom overflowed with 376 visiting correspondents from 50 countries, 166 from Israel itself, diplomats and observers.

Dr. Robert Servotzios, the powerful Nuremberg Trial's defense attorney, personally chosen by Eichmann, didn't deny guilt. Eichmann was either "a small bolt in a large machine," in Servotzios' words, or "one who deeply identified with the cause, *initiating* mass programs of murderous evil," in the prosecution's.

Israel picked up the tab, paying the defense a (for the time record) fee of $30,000, with all expenses paid. Justice would be thorough and expensive. The public balked at its taxes going for this, but that was the policy. Surely, the main goal was airing the Holocaust to the world so that such a thing could never happen again. But, without an execution, the message would get lost. Getting one wouldn't be easy. It had *never* happened before in Israel (nor ever again since).

Over a hundred witnesses testified. Thousands of incriminating Nazi documents, most personally signed by Eichmann, were entered as evidence. But there was a long haul from proving he was a team member to proving that Eichmann was captain. That would be necessary for the death sentence.

Call him a renegade. Call him whatever you want. But a rat is a rat. And it was one of Eichmann's buddies who sold him out and helped do him in. William Zosn, a journalist of German descent and Nazi collaborator, who had also escaped to Argentina, had convinced Eichmann in 1955 to give him a taped interview, a rehashing of good old times. The conversation took place in Buenos Aires.

Friendship is friendship, but money is money. As the trial revved up in Jerusalem, Zosn sold the interview to *Life* magazine, which published it in the November 1960 edition under the headline, *Eichmann's Confession:*

"I regret nothing. It could be that Hitler made mistakes along the way. No one can argue, though, that he paved his own path to the top, from a simple soldier to *der Führer* of 80 million Germans. This success alone sufficed to convince me of the importance to follow him. He was so talented that people knew they were to follow him. I too was happy to feel this talent, and I still justify him.

"I will not embarrass myself, nor show remorse in any form. I must tell the truth—were we successful killing all 10,300,000 Jews, according to Himmler's statistics, living there in

1933, I would have said, 'Excellent, we've destroyed an enemy!'

Zosn asked, "Don't you at all bemoan what was done?"

"Yes," answered Eichmann. "I'm sorry about one thing—that I wasn't more aggressive battling those hindering our work. Look. Now, you see the result—the establishment of a new Jewish state."

The prosecution used this interview to its fullest. The judges drew on it in their verdict, for years quoting it during interviews and referring to it in their memoirs. The Prosecutor, Gideon Hausner had said, "Even a fraction of the evidence entered would suffice to convict him many times over. Much of our effort was aimed at shocking and educating the world with additional revelations."

Finally, near the end of the sixteen-week trial, state prosecutor Hausner's closing statement echoed much of world sentiment:

"I request from this court to deal to this evil-incarnate the just means he deserves. Even were he to die daily, or a thousand-fold a day, this would pale to serve as atonement for the suffering he caused to one innocent child. Man's capability does not suffice to punish Adolph Eichmann sufficiently; neither partially, the sickly evil, the ocean of torment he brought on the Jewish people—even one day of his diabolical work."

"The annihilation of a nation stands before you, enemy of

mankind, spiller of innocent blood."

"I request the death penalty."

Eichmann's corpse was cremated, his ashes scattered over the Mediterranean Sea.

The sound of dripping above my head had been growing stronger, reignited by the burning issue of the diaries. Destroying them was not realistic. The idea of presenting them to the German government to do as it wished appeared in the press. This would extricate Israel from *directly* supplying the sons with their prize, but indirectly, they'd still win.

I scanned the papers daily for those two years. So did my wife, although she wouldn't let me know.

My father-in-law, mother-in-law, Uncles Meir and Simon and Aunt Bertha couldn't allow themselves to show any interest. It would *kill* them.

I believed, hoped, a clever solution would materialize. A wonderfully clever solution, releasing these "important" documents to the inquisitive worlds' eye—*without* rewarding or benefiting the undeserving.

Then one day, Tuesday, February 29, 2,000, headlines in all Israeli papers trumpeted: TOMORROW MORNING EICHMANN DIARIES OPEN TO PUBLIC VIEW IN ISRAELI NATIONAL

ARCHIVES JERUSALEM.

The suffering caused by this man continues, for multitudes, daily. For me, sitting in my office, though, the phantom dripping, at least, has ceased.

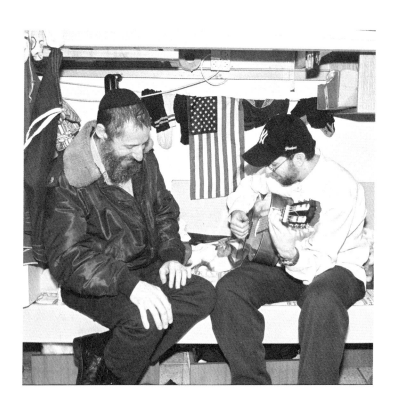

Part II

Maximum Hope

10

Aging With Time

Age positively affects inmates.

Clearly, other factors such as family background and education play a large part in their makeup. Yet, one thing is shared by all—the older the prisoner gets, the more placid, and contemplative he becomes.

Statistically, worldwide, a large proportion of the inmate population consists of repeat offenders, often having served two, three, or more sentences. Recidivism. Crime, evading capture, trial and incarceration have become a way of life.

This is how it works.

Early on, it's a youth-related rush of adventure. Scheming: the conception, planning, surveillance, hushed anticipation, excited conspiracy amongst accomplices, "We'll be in and out in a *snatch*."

Perpetration: adrenaline rush, heart-pounding, high respiration. Splitting the spoils: exultation of success, leading to continued risks. Conclusions: how easy it is to make money this way. How foolish are those becoming gray-haired, prematurely aged with nine-to-five, five-days-a-week, four-weeks-a-month, twelve-months-a-year jobs.

Reaching mid- to late-twenties, criminals start to mellow. Their siblings are celebrating birthdays, bar-mitzvahs for *their* kids, but 'uncle' can't attend. Aging parents can't visit as easily as during earlier stretches: "I don't have the energy, I used to." Grandparents pass away, but inmates are unable to attend the funeral. Still they don't mend their ways. They'll be released, but they'll be back. The fire is still there. You hear it in their voices, see it on their faces, feel it in their deportment.

With early- to mid-thirties, *suddenly,* they're "getting on." Retrospectively, they've spent the last two decades in and out of prison, a revolving door. Brothers and sisters, busy running their own lives, don't have the time—or interest—in him: "I just can't visit this week, I have to take the kids to the dentist," or money for deposits in his commissary accounts. With a shock, the inmate realizes that some accomplices have committed suicide. Many prisoners, too, have attempted—they themselves have perhaps contemplated. The sobering notion starts to bother them: "What is life for?"

The late-thirties hit like a sledgehammer: "I can't believe it! I'm almost forty. I have nothing—no family, no home, nothing." *Now,* the inmates are worrying about their own families. If during this dizzying roller-coaster trip—apprehension, sentencing, sitting, release—they've had children, it painfully dawns on them, "I don't even know my own kids." They miss important events: "Tell Esther daddy can't be at her graduation, but I'll make it up to her," he says, but thinks, *How many times have I said that!?*—and his heart jumps to his throat. Criminals without children awaken agonized to the fact their final chances are rapidly fading. It's nearly impossible to find a mate. Past potential partners are married, irrevocably damaged, or dead from drug overdose. The prisoners are alone. They won't say what they're feeling: *I'm not invincible anymore.*

These are brutal truths to face.

After this age it's very rare for an inmate to continue criminal behavior. They weary of prison routine. They're emptied; exhaustion sets in, homesick—for a home which might not exist.

They open to me. "I've had it. I have to start a family. It's enough." Those words from a prisoner in his late thirties are candid. He won't be back.

Is this exhausting merry-go-round nightmare etched in stone, unalterable once set into motion? Experience shows it is; statistics affirm it. You can't argue with what is. I too feared nothing could be done to stop this imploding, self-destructive descent into dark emptiness.

But, over the years, I have met rare inmates who put a doubt in my mind. In stark contrast to the hustle of prison life, a mixture between a raucous carnival and passing lane on a crowded interstate highway, these particular prisoners glow.

It's a high-energy atmosphere in prison. Everyone is busy: heading out to work detail, cleaning the building, assembling air conditioning parts, getting sent to or returning from court appearances. Constant action, a loud tumultuous scene. As an adaptive mechanism, to better pass the time, many inmates adopt a robot-like facade. There is laughter, backslapping, and macho-hugging, but these are emotionally empty poses. Even aggressive tough-guy behavior and speech are mechanically evolved protective devices, lowering the pressure level, allowing life to continue on a more or less even keel. Life in prison demands going through the motions necessary to survive.

It's against this dark background that one can appreciate interludes of quiet concern, someone acting sincerely, not by rote, breathing a breath of fresh air to those around him.

11

Another Chance

Moshe and I methodically trekked around our expansive complex visiting inmates. His mild manner, endearing glance, and comforting tone did wonders. "Joseph! We're from the same bad neighborhood," he'd say with a voice both prodding and pleading. "Half the neighborhood is here serving time. Is that good? Is that a good way to spend time? Come study with us in the *yeshivah* (religious school). There's coffee and sugar there everyday." To another, "Dave, cheer up. Things will be okay at home. Your brother promised me your family would take care of all the bills, while you're here. Stay strong."

Moshe, 40, personally knows all the other prisoners from his neighborhood in Bat Gan. They grew up together. Low-income, with sky-high illiteracy and divorce rates, rampant with drug dealing, located on the seacoast and bordering Haifa, Bat Gan is one of

Israel's criminal breeding grounds.

A seemingly high proportion of Bat Gan residents are second generation Moroccan Jews. Their parents and grandparents kept a pietistic life-style back in Morocco. All Jews did, back there—that was the way of life.

They began arriving in Israel en masse, in the early 1950s. The fledgling country, declared in existence barely two years earlier, struggled for existence against *seven* hostile surrounding armies. Food was frighteningly scarce, living conditions were horrendous. Absorbing the Moroccan immigration, the population doubled, and Israel found itself with twice as many hungry mouths to feed and jobs to provide. Rural people like Moshe's father couldn't compete with their better educated, multi-lingual European contemporaries. The role models became the local Mafia who easily organized criminal activity among a weakened, provincial population.

Coolly sidestepped, their old-country ideals ignored, their modesty went unappreciated. The humble quietly vanished. Those willing to share their only piece of bread had only the plate left to show for it. Their immigrant fathers formed mini-prayer rooms in the corners of government-allocated apartments, they met in study groups in the small kitchenettes and remained protected in their own pristine world.

Their children were less fortunate. The government forced them to attend public school, where they mixed with children from another world. This generation didn't cope. Many ended up in crime. The prisons brim with second generation Moroccan children. The apple fell far from the tree.

This is Moshe's world. He is family with these unfortunates.

I have no idea how he grew up (his term is for an old count of tax evasion earned running his corner grocery). All I know is that, for the last fifteen years, Moshe has been taking returning to his heritage seriously—and supporting others *very* seriously. Helping seasoned offenders back to the human track, he is plodding but unstoppable.

"Moe, stop being angry," Moshe warmly advised.

Six feet tall and wiry, Moe was constantly fighting, the reason he landed in prison. It had been a senseless drunken fight in a bar at 2:00 A.M. Blades came out. So did his opponent's left eye. Now he fought his roommates—over telephone rights, who calls first.

"Stop, or you'll end up dead," Moshe quietly continued. His peaceful, unassuming demeanor could leave anyone speechless. Moe averted his eyes, shifted his weight, shrugged his shoulders.

"What is it?" Moshe asked.

"Commissary, I want to be first in line..."

"Is that a reason to fight...?" Moshe urged smiling.

Moe said nothing.

Our classes met in a room in the middle floor of the prison, outfitted with six long tables and wooden benches. Inmates appeared at 7:30 A.M. Every morning, Moshe made sure the newer students had a place to sit, the hot water urn was boiling and, through me, that there was enough hot coffee and sugar. We both knew that two things were drawing students to a voluntary program. Celestial, because they came; worldly, because what *kept* them coming was the cup of black coffee.

So, every morning, slapping my buddy, the kitchen officer, on the back, telling him, "It's for a good purpose...," I'd return with kilo bags of coffee and sugar —valuable commodities—and pass them into Moshe's protection.

I have often wondered about the tremendous symbolic significance in prison of a cup of coffee, infinitely much more than a social amenity. By comparison, opening a car door for someone is courteous; saying, "please," pleasant; "thank you," polite. Offering a cup of coffee inside is incomparably more penetrating.

"Make you a cup of coffee?" is an invitation to be seated—to forget where we are. Elsewhere a civil act, in the *uncivil* prison jungle this represents recognition of a man's basic honor, his inalienable self-esteem. A cup of coffee and a smile can save lives.

Beyond our class activities, we worked hard establishing mini-wards devoid of the decadence—profanity, lurid posters, extortion, drug dealing—prevalent elsewhere. We requested allocation of a cell specifically for this purpose and were pleasantly surprised when this cell shortly grew into two. They became comforting shelters, places where prisoners routinely gathered for quiet, intelligent conversations—talks to calm body and soul.

From his own commissary stockpile, or leftover from his prison allocation, Moshe provided cake, fruit, and most importantly, a soothing word for the constant flow of guests.

Late afternoon, after work detail these cells filled, where inmates spoke between themselves, discussed their private thoughts. During Moshe's ten months with us, the interpersonal web of support developed way beyond my expectations.

Often, we accepted borderline students. "Take this guy in," Moshe would say, hopefully. "His head's not really into study, not wholly on straight, but he needs the dollar-a-day student stipend. No one outside is depositing any cash in his commissary account. He'll do his best."

We'd encourage them to come punctually, participate, act conscientiously. When our expectations didn't pan out, I'd call them in for a talk. After a number of times, if I felt there was insufficient cooperation on the inmate's part and his example seemed detrimental, I would suspend his attendance at our program.

Moshe involved himself in all these cases. Quiet when agreeing with me, he'd gently dissent when he didn't. "Give him another chance, I'll talk to him."

The financial situation at home was desperate. Moshe's wife and *eight* children had no income besides a monthly social-benefits payment, which barely covered the rent. I had inside knowledge; we'd discuss it in depth, and I saw his less than elegantly dressed wife during her weekly visits. Often she failed to arrive because she didn't have bus fare.

"Moshe," I said. "There's another prison, not far from here where you can make a little more money." In our prison, he'd been receiving an extremely low amount as my assistant; there it would be a bit more significant.

"I think the most important thing is to take care of your family," I told him. "Make any money you can, and send it."

"How much can I make?"

"I don't know," I answered honestly. "Let's say here you get $20 a month. If you got $300 there, though not a salary by outside standards, I'd take it. It will help your wife. She looked pale in her last visit. That would put some groceries on the table."

"I don't know," he thought out loud. "We're helping so many people here."

"I know," I countered. "But your first responsibility is to

your family."

Obviously torn, he continued, "...on the other hand, there are a lot of people depending on us here."

Eventually, I visited the other institution but discovered the added amount to be trivial. Moshe felt relieved. He would continue helping his fellow inmates, while having to continue soothing his wife and hoping for the best.

The inmate population consistently stood over our building's maximum legal capacity. The Israel Prison Service administration was aware of the chronic overcrowding, which created a constant burden for us, as well as them.

One day, orders arrived directing a large number of inmates to be transferred to another prison, among them Moshe. The orders fell for the next day.

This day was very hectic, and, because of other responsibilities, I barely found a chance to touch base at my own office. The hour of the transfer found me in the hall outside my office. One of our students came running up to me. "Go quickly, Moshe is packed. They're getting ready to transport him."

I hurried to the holding-room, expecting him to be upset. We'd worked hard together, done good things. Who knew where they were taking him? To what conditions? Our prison had been a stable, satisfying place. He was still a prisoner, and, all in all, he had to take care of himself as well.

However, as the guards' raucous yelling and the inevitable clanging of keys and handcuffs drew closer, we both realized that a fruitful, mutually enjoyable situation had suddenly come to a halt. Before entering the police transit, holding his duffel bag in one hand, my arm in the other, Moshe's quietly spoken parting words will stay with me for a long time:

"Listen, two things: coffee and encouragement."

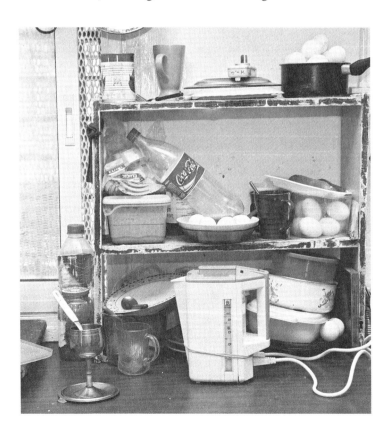

12

Now You're Talking

Earlier, we skirted the rhetorical: "What does the chaplain do all day—what do you actually *do* with them?" because completely answering that would take volumes. Here we'll relate one thing I do do with them, and in the process reveal my best talk.

Chaplains speak. This is their power, the spoken word. In Israel, a country with a predominantly Jewish population, our words are examined microscopically; messages, scrutinized. Many of us, therefore, are thoughtful as to what we say, especially in public.

In prison, by contrast, the intelligence officer's job is to learn which inmates hold grudges against one another and keep them safely distanced. He monitors gang power struggles, keeps tabs on extortion and other power plays. The security officer's job is to make sure no one escapes.

What does the *chaplain* do? Daily, he doesn't prevent escapes, transport supplies, supervise the thrice daily head counts. What does he *do* all day?

We talk.

We encourage devastated inmates deserted by wives whose ebbing patience has finally given out. We patiently counsel distraught staffers with urgent family problems. We typically deliver official addresses at national Soldiers' Memorial Day ceremonies. We officiate at in-house weddings where the groom is restricted from marrying outside the prison. Finally, we eulogize.

It is not an easy job. To prevent escapes? Check the bars a lot. To prevent retaliatory murders? Use planted informers.

But, figuring out what to say hourly, under time pressure, is a monumental challenge.

Teaching is supposed to be a significant part of our day. We're expected not only to supervise other teachers under us, but to instruct personally as well. That's in theory. In practice, hectic prison life, easily likened to a rushing river, doesn't always afford opportunities to instruct. Too often, classroom study programs, once established, quickly get washed away in the current of constant activity.

Experience shows, right after the afternoon prayers is the best bet to get a few words in; gathered, daily chores behind, inmates appreciate hearing a discussion, short talk.

Too often, because of administrative responsibilities, I don't have time to prepare something to say.

Frequently, I ad-lib. Before speaking, I flip through the nearest book for something pertinent, an interesting idea.

Sometimes, I rely on reading cold. This suffices for an informal chat. But, there's a downside. Because, reading to a group has a danger—you may look up and find the flock has flown the coop.

One extremely hectic day during prayers, a thick book of the code of Jewish law, lying on the table, caught my eye. I absentmindedly leafed through its pages mentally noting sections of a relevant subject which could be read straight.

The service ended. I took my regular place at the front of the room, opened the book on the reading stand, cleared my throat and began to read.

The room fell quiet. I continued reading.

Shortly, barely three-quarters down a page, a voice deep down in my mind warned that the room was much too quiet.

This must not be interesting, I thought. They must be exchanging bored glances. Self-conscious, I read faster.

The quiet intensified.

How bad could it be, anyway?

Surprisingly, an inmate asked me to repeat something. Someone was paying attention.

A conversation flared up. Another prisoner asked me to repeat something.

The discussion picked up. We were in the middle of a heated debate.

The talk:

"I'd like to share with you some interesting laws which happened to have caught my eye," I said. "I found some of this interesting, thought you'd enjoy it."

"Let's start," I continued, and began reading, "'Unjustified physical assault, an act which transgresses rulings spanning the historical gamut of legal literature, is correspondingly viewed with utmost severity. Numerous prominent decisions label the perpetrator liable before contact, from demonstration of intent, e.g. taunting his weapon, raising his fist.'"

I continued reading, "Even, violent *speech* should be avoided. 'The words of the wise are transmitted quietly.'"

Until this point the room had remained very quiet—too—in fact. My suspicions began to itch.

"Next: 'Entering someone's home without permission is forbidden. The home owner is allowed to remove such an unwanted trespasser using force if necessary and there are no alternatives.'"

A chilling silence descended into the room, electricity stung through the air.

Something just happened, I thought.

"Here's one," I continued. "'If someone catches a thief breaking into his home he is permitted to use physical violence stopping him. From nightfall, potentially lethal force is permitted, the assumption: the offender, keenly aware of the likely peril, comes prepared for anything to secure safe escape. The home owner may use, therefore, equal and necessary force."

The second those words left my mouth, it hit me: What was I thinking, reading *this* to *them*?

Sam, a tall, lanky happy-go-lucky type interjected, "That's not exact. Fact is, most night-burglars prefer operating unarmed; all you can get is two to four. Carrying an illegal weapon can get you six."

"What you talkin' about?" Aaron, a repeat felon with a court record two feet long, indignantly retorted. "You remember that tough old judge in Haifa, with the thick black glasses? I forget his name. Anyhow, in '92 he slapped me with five and six months for breaking and entering. Didn't let me open my trap the entire trial."

A big hulky guy, with thick hairy arms and a wide, ugly scarred face, seated in the front row, thought that was hilarious, began laughing, his body jerking back and forth, and banging the table with his fists. Turning around, still chuckling, he sized Aaron up slowly from top to bottom, drawing out with feigned drama, "He gave you five and a half because you're so pretty. Ha, ha, ha." Everyone broke into laughter.

I watched disbelieving, silent. A discussion broke out. It was amazing to experience. It was like a pot-luck dinner. Everyone had a personal experience to share.

Aaron chirped in, looking at me, "One of my buddies is a day guy..."

"Meaning?"

"He does, how could we say this, not exactly invited housecalls, when everyone's out."

Great, I thought, *that's considerate.*

"Once," Aaron continued, "the owner returned unexpectedly."

I listened.

"Yup, drove up the driveway, got out, walked up to his own front door, my friend inside."

"What happened then?" I asked, my curiosity stirred.

"It was nuts, the guy's standing there, hears moving around inside his own home."

"What did he do?" I asked, really interested. "What did your buddy do?—And, how did you know this story so well, anyhow?"

"I happened to be outside..."

Oh no, I thought.

"The owner put his ear to the door, pulled a pistol from under his shirt, put the key in the lock, quietly opened the door."

The anticipation in the room tightened.

"Then?" I asked for everyone.

"Five minutes went by, I happened to be in the backyard..."

'Happened,' I thought, *gimme a break.*

"Okay, okay, so what happened?"

"I heard the owner yell, a shot went off..."

You could hear a feather fall, we were all ears.

"Then," Aaron stopped, took a dramatic breath, "my buddy went soaring out the open back window, his foot got caught on the sill, he fell onto his head, rolled over, beat it outta there before the guy made it to the window."

Before the silence wore off, tree-trunk arm inmate broke in, "That was *you* out that window. You heisted a cop's joint, without staking it out... Ha! Ha! Ha!"

Exploding laughter in the room.

Eventually, the conversation returned to the law. "But," Sam continued, looking at me, "like I said—you can't assume a burglar enters thinking about defending himself till death. Personally, I always have a clear escape route—otherwise, I'd just give up. Forget weapons."

Then the questions came. They asked me to review the legal

distinctions between burglary: during the day from at night; in the home of an acquaintance as opposed to a stranger's home; apprehending the burglar entering or leaving; with or without witnesses. The pages turned back and forth, we researched, discussed, the conversation heated up—everybody was involved.

Time escaped us. Two *hours* had transpired. Our concentration was only shattered when the PR system blared, "All inmates are to return to their wards. Dinner is being distributed."

That afternoon, I realized something which changed forever how I prepare to speak in public. A universal truth, one I'll take with me for a long while.

A good talk should always, *always*, begin with a subject which interests the audience.

13

A Eulogy

When an inmate's father passed away, I became the perfect choice to act as escorting officer to the cemetery: As an officer, I had the necessary rank, as chaplain I fit the role. Seated in my office, at exactly 12:00 noon, I received a phone call from the security officer: "Get ready to escort a prisoner to his father's funeral. You've got three guards, and a driver. Come to my office for orders."

It was a hot summer day. I expected the van's air-conditioner to be on one of its off-days. I also expected cramped seating and bumper-to-bumper Tel Aviv afternoon traffic. Besides the discomfort and hassles traveling, I'd be expected to deliver a eulogy once there. In general, I avoid doing eulogies. I'm just not good at them. Doing one about someone I've never met is a nightmare.

I waited at the front gate for our mourning prisoner to be

brought down. He was an inmate I didn't know personally.

"Rabbi!" he said, as soon as he saw me. "Great! You're escorting officer." I knew what he was going to ask.

"I'd like us to stop by my home on the way to the cemetery," he continued. "That shouldn't be a problem. Right?" I suspected he was more excited about the trip than upset about his father's passing.

"I'll ask the security officer and see what he says," I said, knowing perfectly well what he'd say. And he did, as soon as I got him on the line. "Your route is from here to the cemetery and back!"

"Repeat that, please," I requested, turning up the phone's speaker. "I said, he's got permission to attend his father's burial. Period. *Not* to visit home and return with contraband."

The guards handcuffed and attached a leg-clamp over the inmate's left knee, bolting the lower part of his thigh to his upper calf. This type of lock, which restricts knee movement, is worn inconspicuously under the clothing during excursions.

We walked out to the van. The driver and another guard got into the front seat. Two hopped into the back. I slid open the side door to the middle seat. The prisoner, of course, couldn't step up into the vehicle. To get in, he put his backside onto the edge of the seat, using his unshackled leg to back-step up and shimmy in. We closed the door.

There was only a foot of space between us and the metal bars separating our compartment from the driver's. Barely enough room, the inmate's leg got wedged diagonally into an impossible angle. "I'm gonna break my leg!" he yelled. The only solution was putting it *onto* the seat, which we did—in the process, wedging *me* into the door. My left hip was jammed into the window handle. "Can't you move?" I complained. "This handle is killing my side!"

"Sorry," he lied, "I have problems of my own."

The van began rolling. I had hoped for some quiet to compose the eulogy. That wouldn't come, though shortly the inevitable did. "I'm so happy you're the escorting officer," my seating partner whined. "Tell the driver to go past my house."

"You already heard the security officer," I said.

"It's my father's funeral," he said, adopting a forlorn

expression. "Come on, I have to be there for my mother. Radio the warden."

"We have orders," I said. "And, if you really care about your mother, stay out of prison," I said.

"A lesson in morals! My family is grieving. What kind of rabbi..."

Two miserable hours later, we arrived. None of his family had. We waited. The temperature was a hot and humid 97° F. With nowhere in sight to buy a cold drink, I took a long swig of warm water from a hose. The moisture only ran through my skin, covering me with a thick layer of perspiration.

By 5:30, we were still alone. Suddenly, a bus full of people showed up. Some cars. Three more buses. *A lot of people came to show their respects,* I thought.

I noticed something disturbingly familiar about a couple dozen men—the clothes, gold chain necklaces, the walk. They debarked from the buses, greeted the guards, handshaking, backslapping. Our prisoner's neighborhood buddies—ex-inmates—were enjoying a reunion with the guards!

Frankly, my mood was lousy. If not for this ceremony, I'd be home, taking a refreshing shower. The perspiration dried on my back, but my hip still throbbed. But, my main problem was I still knew absolutely nothing about the one I'd be speaking about—something I'd take care of promptly.

I ordered our three armed guards to watch the prisoner, then went fact-finding.

I introduced myself to a young man standing nearby, asking if he could tell me a few things about the deceased: his name, something about his family. He said the departed's name was Saul. The family? He motioned with his head in the direction of two dapper, well-decked fellows—ex-inmates. The genetic similarities to our prisoner were striking—these were his brothers. I asked what Saul had done for a living. He replied, "The apple doesn't fall far from the tree..."

To say I was running out of time and groping for material would be an understatement. I scouted for someone else, and noticed something odd. Here and there, throughout the cemetery grounds, were individuals and couples, who stood out: very well dressed, professional types. People who carried an educated demeanor.

I approached one such couple and said, "Could you tell me something about Saul?"

"Yes," the fellow replied humbly. His wife lowered her head, averted her glance. "I...suppose..."

"Okay..." I nudged.

"In the neighborhood...he...took...kids..." he motioned with his head to the other atypicals, lowered his voice and continued, "under...his...wing..."

What the...? I wondered.

"My father was constantly in trouble with the law. In and out of jail," the gentleman continued laboriously. It was clearly painful for him to admit all this. "My mother tried supporting us. Not an easy task, seven kids, two rooms..."

You seem, it dawned on me, *to have done okay.*

"I was in the streets, most of the time, from eleven years of age..."

I continued my rounds.

The outdoor loudspeaker barked, directing our band towards the enclosed courtyard where the remains are placed during the final farewell. We clumsily meandered over: weeping women, family, loud children, a crew of ex-inmates, in the center a hand- foot-cuffed inmate, surrounded by armed guards.

We entered the courtyard, the sobs and shouting died down, the cluster settled into place. Somebody hushed, "Quiet, the rabbi is going to speak."

I approached the podium, glanced at the deceased wrapped in a prayer shawl, according to tradition, then around at waiting faces.

"We're gathered here to honor the deceased. In the name of the Prison Service, I'd like to convey condolences to the family. He has given, He has taken. May your family know only good tidings from here on. Stay strong and united."

"I didn't personally know the deceased, Saul. But this afternoon I have met a number of people who did. Some of them have been affected deeply by him. They have shown a willingness to say a few words." I nodded to the first fellow I'd met. He approached the podium.

Unused to speaking publicly, he waited for my nod of encouragement to begin. He related how Saul had called him aside as a fifteen year old. The gentleman explained how his own father had had problems with the law, until he passed away prematurely at forty. Saul, saw the teenager, devastated by his loss, wavering between good friends and friends who nothing good would come from. He described how Saul had leveled with him: "It's your life. But, remember, you eat what you cook. Look at me. In and out of prison. Is that the life you want? To never know if you're speaking with a friend or police informant? Where you'll be spending the night? Or, a good family, stability?"

Saul also supplied the answers: "Stay in school. Do your prayers every day. Stay away from bad friends." But Saul did more. He spoke with the boy constantly when he was free. He even kept on him by phone—from prison.

Then spoke Shimon, a local cop, and boxing instructor who thought he was tough until Saul slapped some sense into him in front of his buddies saying, "You're too smart to end up like me." There were others, a housewife, a bus driver.

As I listened, I wondered if Saul's inability to tear himself away from the routine of his life, or save his own sons, added to his resolve to help others.

My knockout punch, though, was Deborah, a woman who immediately commanded respect. In her mid-fifties, she had a calculated determination, an aura of authority. Deborah was also very well known. She was the local high school principal.

"I was sixteen," she began. "One day, on my way home from school, Saul saw me on the street. He asked me if I was Dan's sister. I said yes. He asked me to meet him the following afternoon outside his home. I agreed. When I got there, he was waiting with a photo album. He showed it to me: shots of his family, bar-mitzvahs, birthday parties. He asked me if I saw anything unusual. I said no. He told me to look again. I still saw nothing. I was young, it looked like any album. We had one at home.

"Finally, Saul looked me squarely in the eye and said, 'I'm not *in* any of those photos.'

"Then, he asked me if my family does things like those activities together. I answered that of course we did. He asked me if everyone attends. I said, of course. He asked me how many siblings we had. I said, five. And, he pressed further: if one did not come to any of these functions, how would the family feel? I was starting to feel frightened, I didn't know what he wanted. Then he made the most powerful statement of my life.

"Saul said, 'Deborah. You're a smart girl. If you want your family to stay together, watch your younger brother, Dan. He's into bad things.' "

"From that day on, I watched Dan with four eyes," Deborah continued. "I made sure he did his homework and didn't wander around late at night.

"Saul, correctly, had told me not to rely on my parents' intervention. They had their hands full just paying the bills. I threw myself head first into my new responsibility. Thank God, Dan completed high school, got married, created a family, and supports himself respectfully.

"That's not all. That experience set me down a path. I attained my teachers' certification. And, twenty years ago, became high school principal.

"It was the satisfaction I got from doing that which made me decide to dedicate my life to *other* peoples' younger brothers and sisters."

I stood listening next to the podium while Deborah spoke. This was the best eulogy I'd ever heard. Not only because it was said naturally, but because it was real.

Ultimately, I don't know if and to what degree the audience was moved. You never know. I'm sure a few of the older people were. Perhaps, some of the younger ones were assessing themselves, if only for that brief moment.

I wonder if Saul helped these people on the spur of the moment to soothe his conscience. Or, did he know he was setting them on the right path for life?

14

Boris

Boris, 6' 4", 240 pounds of hulking muscle, in his late forties, stood poised in front of me. He had a huge head set on a broad, powerful, muscular thick-boned torso. No bodily movement when he spoke; he just held you fixed with his steady glare, seemingly ready for a fight. Etched on his face was the intense ruthless expression of a killer.

How did I meet Boris?

A few years ago I spent Yom Kippur, the holiest day of the Jewish calendar, in one of my prisons. The idea sprang from necessity. The cantors scheduled to lead the services, didn't show up. There's a budget for this; officers are not expected to spend their holidays with the prisoners. But, no cantors—no services.

So, there I was. My wife, Miriam, packed the traditional

knee-length, white gown worn on this day, slippers of man-made material (leather is considered too comfortable to wear on this atonement day), and ram's horn, blown as a sign of the fast day's completion.

I arrived at the prison the afternoon preceding the holiday and made sure all the preparations were taken care of. In expectation of larger prisoner participation, the dining hall had been converted into a makeshift synagogue, including the construction of a 'holy ark' in which to place the Torah scrolls. The prayer books were in place. The room was orderly and sparkling.

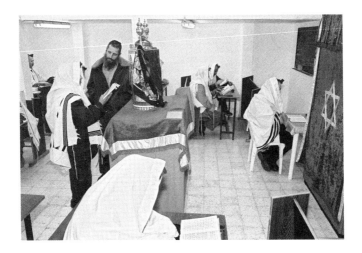

An hour before the holiday began, I made my rounds of the cells to wish the inmates an easy fast and a healthy new year.

It was then I met Boris, a mountain of a man, standing there in the middle of his cell, in all his awesome might, dressed only in his underwear.

"*Du redtz Yiddish?* You speak Yiddish?" he asked, explaining his Hebrew wasn't too good.

"*Yuh,*" I answered.

We shook hands. I patted him on the shoulder, gave him a smile.

He warmed up. An inkling of a smile slowly, but only briefly, passed his lips. Nodding, he grunted to the other prisoners, "*Er iz beseder*, he's okay." A pass straight out of a mafia family meeting.

Covering his huge beefy shoulder was a large, eight-by-seven inch tattoo. It depicted an old Jew with a long white beard, wearing a fur hat; kneeling on one knee, he held both ends of a sword horizontally above his head. Resting on top of the sword's top edge was a large Star of David.

"I'm Russian," he said.

"Why the tattoo?" I asked.

"I'm a Jew. And I want everyone to know. Especially, those lousy Russians," he said, then jerked his left arm up from the elbow placing his right fist in the inner part of the bent elbow (the Israeli equivalent of an expletive). "Animals, filth, *goyim*! (non-Jews)" he muttered, turning the sides of his mouth down in disgust.

"I'm also a *Cohen*," (historically, the priests, an unbroken paternal line to Moses' older brother, Aaron), he said proudly, making the famous hand sign with which they pronounce blessings.

"Do you know anything about the religion?" I asked.

"Nothing at all." Then he laughed, a kind of bellowing, raspy blast, with his whole body, a laugh that expressed humor, hidden suffering, fear, fierce resolution.

His ethnic pride was sincere and refreshing.

Later, during the holiday, I asked him what he did for a living in Russia. Stammering, he muttered, "A *gonif*, a thief."

"How long have you been in prisons?"

"In and out," he said, "for over twenty-seven years."

I started to get the picture.

"What's it like in Russian prisons?" I continued. "I heard it's much harder than elsewhere."

"The guards aren't like here," he said, his body heaving with laughter. Then, suddenly, a cold heaviness shot through his eyes, "Here the guards are human... There not."

"What was it like?"

"You don't want to know," he said slowly, thinking. "They give you dry bread, water, potatoes. That's all you eat. You're always hungry. You can't talk to anyone all day."

"What did you do to spend time?"

"For years, we broke heavy boulders with huge

sledgehammers for eight hours a day. The authorities took these by railroad cars and dumped them into the sea."

"What?!" I asked disbelieving.

"The imprisonment is to break the spirit. That's their tactic."

"Did anyone ever escape?" I asked.

He laughed, belting out that explosive sound. "From *Siberia*?" Then he remembered. "Once I was in a camp, not far from the cities, a day's train ride, a week's walk. My bunkmates escaped. Took a guard with them."

"Why?" I asked, but knew I shouldn't.

His body tightened,"For food."

My stomach turned. I took a deep breath, exhaled slowly.

"How did they look at Jews in prison?" I asked.

"They don't," he said, penetrating me with a look I never saw before, a piercing glance in which I felt a fierce coldness, which could only be connected with death itself. "They kill the weaker ones."

"Who?"

"Russian thugs. Only the strongest survive in Russian prisons, especially when it comes to Jews."

"How did *you* survive all those years with that tattoo in Russian prisons?"

His lips formed a smile his eyes did not. I shuddered.

Here was a Jew, by his own admission totally ignorant of any of his history or inner meaning, yet proud enough to flaunt a huge picture depicting an ethnically defiant theme, a tattoo which, were it not for his size, probably would have gotten him killed.

"Where you ever attacked?"

"Yes," he said, lifting his shirt, showing me a five inch scar above his kidney."

"What...?"

"One, in front, with a shovel, another behind me with a knife."

"And...?"

"The one in front, I killed. Then I collapsed. Woke up in the infirmary."

"Anyone punished?"

A sudden laugh. "In Russian prisons, no one talks. We fight. One wins. One loses. Guards don't care."

All during Yom Kippur, Boris kept flashing into my mind. His personality intrigued me.

During the closing services, as customary, I gave a speech. I spoke about the Cantonists in Russia. These were Jewish children, kidnapped by government order for forced military service. The background was a list of laws of unfathomable cruelty enacted between the years 1825-1855, under the regime of Czar Nikolai I. The harshest was the Cantonist law under which Jewish boys were conscripted, at *eight years of age,* for a *twenty-five year* service, to the Russian army. With any hint of approaching Russian soldiers, the Jews hastily hid their children. Inevitably, many were kidnapped. The number ran in the tens of thousands.

Many of these captive youth managed to stay together, fearing the worst, practicing whatever they remembered of their religion. Some were beaten mercilessly by their officers. Many died bitter deaths.

Once a group of rabbis came to Petrograd (the capital of Russia) for a convention, asking special permission from the military authorities to spend Yom Kippur with a group of these youths. The request was granted. Approaching the last prayer, *Neila* ("closing," referring to the gates of heaven), the rabbis suggested that one of the boys be honored with the concluding opening of the holy ark. The Cantonists unanimously selected one of their group, a quiet eleven year old named Yosef.

The reason for this choice wasn't apparent, but it would be.

"Open your shirt," they told him. He did, revealing a mass of deep scars, cuts and bruises from years of punishment.

Yosef approached the prayer post, opened the ark. With the assembly looking on, he cleared his voice and in a clear calm tone addressed his Maker.

"Almighty. During *Neila* Jews pray for *gezunt,* health, during the coming year. Look at my beaten, broken body. I don't think of requesting health. Jews pray for wealth. Look at me. Possessing wealth doesn't even occur to me. Unmarried Jews pray for a mate," he stopped momentarily, holding back tears, "but who would ever take me, after all that I've been through?

"All I ask you, my G-d, G-d of my parents and their fathers, is grant me the power this coming year to remain a proud Jew. And to sanctify Your holy Name."

With this he began the mourner's prayer, "*Yisgadol yeyiskadosh Shmeh rabbah...* Exalted and hallowed be His great Name throughout the world which He created..."

Then, in this most dramatic moment of the Jewish year, the words just came to me. "It's written, 'The Al-mighty wants the *heart* of man.' It's not only our minds, but our hearts the Al-mighty wants," I explained.

"I think it would be fitting for Boris to open the ark." Then, with warm, uncontrollable tears flowing down my cheeks, I invited Boris to honor us by coming up front and opening the holy ark.

Everyone nodded in agreement.

Boris gratefully accepted the invitation, but had no idea why he was being honored.

15

Agunah!

Agunah: a wife deserted by her husband without a divorce. By Jewish law a wife must obtain a divorce scroll (a *get*) from her husband before remarrying. (The law applies to husbands as well.) As the first chaplain for the only women's prison in Israel, Neve Tirzah, I saw firsthand what a terrible catastrophe being an *agunah* is, trapping women in marriages that don't exist.

Neve Tirzah was filled with such women.

Inmate Sarah Baron asked to speak with me. A pleasant woman, maybe thirty years old, she entered my office, barely holding back tears. She trembled as she spoke. She and her husband had been expatriate Israelis living in California. Sarah had been trying to get a divorce for three years.

"Why?" I asked.

She wouldn't say exactly. She just spoke about a terrible "home" environment and bad influences present around the clock.

I guessed David had involved himself in illegal things. Subsequent research proved me right. He headed a drug and porno ring from the home. I figured the American legal authorities would catch up with him, but they hadn't. Yet.

Without telling her husband, Sarah fled with the two children -- Rachel, 7, Michael, 5 -- to her parents in Israel. With no funds, she foolishly took with her seven pounds of hashish, hoping its sale would ease the burden on her father and mother until she could get settled. Apprehended for possession and transport, she was tried and sentenced to eight months. I didn't really see her as a drug-trafficker.

"The children are with your parents?"

"Yes. But..."

"Go on."

Sarah put her head in her hands; sobs racked her thin frame. I heard her moan, a sound as old as motherhood itself.

"Take it easy. It will be all right."

"He... arrived... in Israel... today. He's... going... to... take... the... children... away..."

And, as things looked now, he had that right. What's legal isn't always just, however, and I thought there must a be a way to help Sarah. She calmed slightly. "Leave it to me," I said. "I'll do my best to help."

"But what can you do?"

"What *you* can do is call your parents. Have them tell David you want him to visit you here. Make sure I'm present when he does."

Alone in my office, I called my boss. "Rabbi Levin, I have a prisoner headed towards becoming an *agunah* real soon if we don't do something. The husband just arrived from the States and isn't wasting time. He's determined to take the two small children back with him, and, if he does, I doubt she'll ever see them or him again. She'll also never get a divorce." I paused for breath. "Correct me if I'm wrong. Doesn't the rabbinical court have jurisdiction to issue a restraining order forbidding a husband from leaving the country in cases of possible *agunah*s?"

"Correct. Where are they from in Israel?"

"Haifa."

"Call the rabbinic court there. Tell them the problem. Fax it."

My fingers were typing the second I hung up.

A few minutes later I telephoned Haifa. I heard the connection being made, and another voice on the line. "Shalom. This is Rabbi Dan, court secretary. What can I do for you?"

"This is Rabbi Jacobs. I'm the rabbi of Neve Tirzah. One of

our inmates is headed towards becoming an *agunah*. I'd like your court to place a restraining order on the husband for all ports of exit until things can be straightened out. I've already sent a fax to this effect."

"I'll see right to it."

The wheels of justice don't have to grind slowly, I thought, if you know who to contact.

The next morning I met Sarah and David in my office at Neve Tirzah, and he was exactly as I'd expected: alligator shoes, tight pants, greasy slicked back hair. I wondered why so many Middle Eastern immigrants dressed like Elvis Presley.

For an hour, I mainly listened and kept watch for violence as they fought it out. Thinking he held all the aces, David was mainly calm, haughty, arrogant. "I'm taking the kids," he stated emotionlessly. "You're in prison, obviously unfit to be a mother. We have time to talk about a divorce. First get out of prison, then come and look for me in California."

My ears pricked. I didn't like any of this.

Sarah alternated antagonism with pleading. "You don't really want the kids," she said. "You just want to spite me. Control." I thought that seemed logical. Besides, her crime was pennies compared to this guy. He just hadn't gotten caught.

"David," I interjected softly. "There's a restraining order preventing you from leaving the country until this dispute is resolved."

"It was served on me last night." He smirked. "If you weren't a rabbi, I'd tell you where to put it. I've already talked to my lawyer in California. He's getting it lifted. He says it's a matter of time for it to be dissolved."

David needed a dose of reality, and I thought he might take it better if he didn't feel the need for bravado and posturing in front of his wife. "David, could we step into another room for a second?"

Once I got him alone, I said, "Listen," looking hard into his eyes. "The advice you're getting is bad. You might think you're going to fly into the wide blue with your children, leaving Sarah's life in ruins, but it's not going to happen. If your lawyer is half as good as you say, he surely knows this by now. If you persist, you're going to be here a long time. Guess you haven't heard of Yehia, who just passed away, still incarcerated after fifteen years for refusing, against court orders, to give his wife a divorce. Are you that stubborn?"

"What kind of country has laws like this?"

"What kind of man would do this to his wife?"

"I'm leaving," he said. "My lawyer will make you wish you'd never been born unless you back off."

I smiled and saw him off.

David would soon find that no place was safe for him. California authorities had him under investigation. Of course, he'd learn that what I'd told him about his prospects in Israel represented the unvarnished truth. And, his "business" needed him; others had started to take it over.

He could try to flee. He might even succeed, but surely not with the two children in tow. He hinted at this when he called me, a week after our first meeting, to appeal to have the restraining order lifted. Such a move would still leave Sarah an *agunah.*

"There are people," I told him, "whose profession is tracking down husbands. They travel all over the world, and almost always return to Israel with signed divorces. We call them modern knights."

David asked how long a divorce would take. When I told him that scheduling an initial hearing in rabbinical court usually took three months, he exploded. To make him angrier, I said, "The second hearing would come two months after the first. Then there's lots of red tape..."

"I can't stay here for five months. I've got business responsibilities back home."

I dug the knife deeper. "You're not listening to me. You'll likely be here much longer than five months. You're not counting the red tape and the bureaucracy."

"My lawyer..."

"Will charge you a lot of money and not accomplish a thing."

"Is there anything you can do to speed this up?"

"Maybe." I paused.

"Well?"

"You'll have to sign a divorce agreement that's fair to Sarah."

"What's fair? She's convicted on a hashish rap! I'm clean as a hound's tooth!"

"Why don't you think it over? No one's going anywhere for now."

I hung up and evaluated Sarah's position. It was strong but not overwhelming. He couldn't take the children but probably could leave her as an *agunah*. He didn't want those kids, but revenge—which is what he really wanted—for her having left him might be within his reach. I had to proceed confidently but remain aware of the dangers.

I talked to Sarah. David had a sister and brother-in-law in California who loved little Rachel and Michael and might be willing to keep them. Calls to the U.S. assured me such was the case. We worked out generous visitation rights for Sarah, including summers in Israel. As far as permanency, I suspected the positions of Sarah and David would soon reverse - he in prison, she on the outside, and making a fruitful life. "I think it's just a matter of time before you have your children back," I told her.

When David called me (I never contacted him - I never

wanted him to think we were anxious), I said I had divorce papers I wanted him to sign.

"I suppose she gets my money."

"She doesn't want your money."

"What if I don't sign?" I could tell from his voice that he was weary of this fight.

"We've been over this before. Do you want to end up like Yehia?"

"I'll come and look over the papers. You better not have given her the store."

I phoned my friend in the Haifa rabbinate, Rabbi Halperin, and explained the problem: if a divorce wasn't obtained in record time, there might be no divorce at all.

"No sweat," he said. "Bring them to the court tomorrow."

The next day, David whined and blustered, but what "out" did he have? He signed the divorce papers. We drove in separate cars (Sarah, two guards, and I in one, he in the other) to Haifa. We made up the divorce papers, which the judges made official. It had been quite a scramble to get permission for Sarah to leave the prison.

We stood in the hallway as the scribe prepared the divorce scroll, which by Jewish law must be handwritten. "I have to get back," David said. "When will the restraining order be lifted?"

"The minute the scroll is prepared."

"It'll feel great to get out of this country."

I didn't tell him it would feel great to have him out.

A few minutes later, it was over, the fastest divorce in Israeli history: less than three hours from the court opening the file to the final decree.

Fortunately, some stories do have happy endings. Sarah still lives in Israel, remarried (to a medical doctor) with two more children. Rachel and Michael also reside in Israel, where they attend a university. The last I heard, David's home was San Quentin Prison.

16

Home

On Sunday, August 4, 1996, between 4:30 and 4:45 in the morning two convicted terrorists executed a brazen escape from one of Israel's most maximum security prisons. This single act changed the entire composition of our prison overnight. And drove home to me the tremendous impact of our program on the prisoners.

The scene was Oshmoret Prison, 15 minutes north of Tel Aviv. It was here the world's most dangerous terrorists were being held inside inescapable walls.

The groundwork for the escape, of Geshan Mahmud with 11 out of 17 years left to serve, and Toupik Ahmad with 4 years out of 12 years, was laid with the decision to begin renovations in the ward holding these terrorists. Ahmad and Mahmud got access to building equipment capable of breaking through concrete. They managed to smuggle these into their ground floor cell. They pried up two square floor tiles under the sink, and molded a perfectly similar block of tiles as a replaceable cover. Over a period of a few months, they assiduously dug through the building's thick cement foundation, boring deeper into the soft earth below, finally leveling off to dig a fourteen-yard-long horizontal tunnel, sneaking right beneath the unsuspecting noses of the vicious security dogs, to the outside world.

The getaway diameter was an amazing *eighteen* inches. The escapees-in-training shed tens of pounds to squeeze through. Displacement of dirt and debris had to be accomplished without arousing suspicion (flushed through the toilet and shower). It was a plan straight out of the books. They were lucky the tunnel didn't collapse on them.

The Prison Commissioner publicly announced, "There will be a full investigation. I will assume complete responsibility if found directly responsible or negligent." Satirical caricatures appeared in the national papers depicting a soon-to-be-announced project: "Oshmoret Subway Station." Morale could have been better.

The day after the escape, prison service high-brass ordered the remaining terrorists of Oshmoret to be exchanged with that same number of inmates from my prison—within 24 hours. The aim was disorientation, and disruption of any additional plans under way.

"We don't want to stir up the prisoners," our security officer explained. "No details are to be repeated until the morning of transfer."

That evening, I told my current assistant, David, to direct our students to get their stuff out of the classroom, get packed.

"What is this all about?" he asked, his brow creased, eyes radiating concern. "Tell me. You know these guys depend on our program."

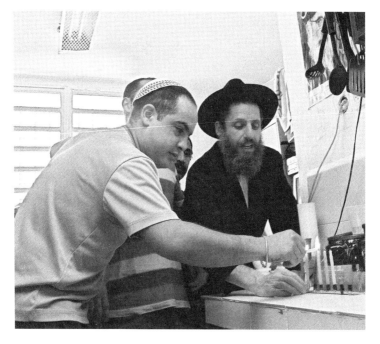

Indeed, during the previous half year, we had extended our influence many fold. Our students made rounds, daily offering to put on *tefillin* with an average of ninety prisoners, a large number considering many did so independently. Many inmates joined rehab, others hooked up with discussion groups to rid themselves of the criminal mind. Our program had been allocated a few eight-bed cells, a rare commodity in a crowded world, as in-house outreach/emergency centers.

David hit it on the nose: "In the jungle, you need a quiet corner to invite guys for a cup of coffee, to chew over what's bothering them." Inmates brought their meager personal supplies of wafers, and fruits to share with less fortunates.

David, 49, sentenced to seven years for tax evasion, altruistically and repeatedly avoided transfer to better conditions.

People like David come from troubled neighborhoods. They feel obliged to prevent others from returning to prison. Whatever ward we're visiting, they call each other by first name, embrace, deride each other for getting into trouble with the law.

Such grassroots communication is superior to anything a professional—someone who never had trouble with the law, did drugs, or experienced firsthand the desolation of an empty life could offer.

The fast-approaching displacement decree struck my students with fear.

The next morning I arrived at work early and reviewed the transport printout. One was David's personal protege', Joseph

Ronen, 35, single though seeing someone seriously. He and David had grown up together. He became one of our successes, David's pride.

At 8:00 A.M. those on the list were ordered, "Ready to move by 9:30."

Joseph wept.

Catching the warden in the corridor outside his cell, he beseeched, "Please, try to keep me here...I'll be alone where they're sending us."

Joseph's entreaties made an indelible impact on me. I knew he never had a stable family or a roof over his head. We were the father he barely knew, family. His hope.

It was impossible to rescind the orders.

"We'll do our best to bring you back, when things quiet down," we promised. "I'll try to visit you," I said.

It isn't fair, I realized, *to think this is just another job, another prison term, another day.* For a lot of people, it's home.

A year and a half following this episode, I was informed by David, that Joseph, now a free man, has married the woman who waited for him during his internment and is leading a quiet life, running a butcher shop in a small Israeli village.

17

Reflections at 3:00 A.M.

My personal rule is that all writing is done at home. This is the only chapter I've written in prison.

I am presently alone on a below-ground floor. It is 3:00 a.m. on a June Friday morning. This floor, albeit eerily empty now, is extremely busy during daytime hours. It has two corridors, each approximately 40 yards long, which meet to form a T-junction. This basement houses five classrooms, a couple of offices, a work space where around sixty prisoners assemble components for air conditioners, and our synagogue, where I am writing these words.

I have been reading here for a few hours.

Not a sound can be heard on this level, or, for that matter, in the entire building.

Until tomorrow at noon, I am on duty, fulfilling my

monthly obligation as officer in charge.

This afternoon, a prisoner expelled from his ward was placed in an isolation cell on the main floor. Due to his irritating ranting, banging on the cell door, and simple space considerations, he was told to move to an adjacent cell. He violently opposed.

Legally limited in their use of force, it took four big guards fifteen loud dramatic minutes to handcuff and relocate him. The agitating ruckus and his self-incurred suffering all seem a distant memory in comparison to the soothing stillness of the present hour.

My nightly inspection brought me to a security ward, where forty convicted terrorists are being held. Glancing at their prison terms, averaging three life sentences each, I shuddered. To receive such sentences they must have murdered that many people—often their own for collaborating with Israeli security forces. Cold-blooded criminals, their entire adolescent life had been dedicated to violence in the name of religion. Now they are behind bars. And it's dead silent and tranquil. At 3:00 A.M. everyone is equal in jail—terrorists, rapists, murderers, deadbeats, tax-evaders.

As the seasonal temperature and humidity rise, so does the violence. Giving class this morning, I tried to dismiss the howling in the corridor, but it only grew. I went outside the classroom to find a group of thirty prisoners mobbing around two fighting convicts rolling around on the floor. I helped some guards separate them.

"What's it about?" I asked a bystander.

"Nothing."

It's hot, tempers flare. In prison, anywhere, people get hurt, maimed for life, killed because of petty arguments. Because of the heat. Because that's what a jungle is.

But now it's 3:00 in the morning and the hushed tranquility in the entire facility accents the foolishness of it all. The hour forces tempers to sleep, all seven hundred of them.

Earlier at 1:30 A.M., during cell-inspection rounds of our criminal wards, my flashlight beam briefly illuminated the serene sleeping faces.

Some lay on their backs, others in a fetal position.

One inmate, who I did not recognize personally, caught my eye—his face was narrow and drawn, he had just a stubble of an unshaven beard. I don't know how a lifetime fit into my thoughts of the next three seconds. *He looks like an innocent child.*

His eyelids were gently closed; facial muscles, relaxed; lips, content; outstretched posture, carefree.

He was once a child.

Did his mother cradle him, tell him he smelled good after his bath? Did she tickle him? Did he giggle? Did she whisper with him his late-night prayers? Sit on his bedside, stroke his face, kiss him goodnight, telling him he was loved? Were those the memories behind this face, at peace with itself?

The beam averted, darkness returns to his unknowing face. I remained struck, pondering.

Then, a fed, bathed, carefree, tucked-in child. Full of the simple joy of life. Felt loved by all, loving all. Brimming with energy and dreams. A life of hope to do good things.

Now, a life of hell. Battles, real or postured, for turf, status. Axes to grind, planning, worries. A distraught, battled existence.

What happened in the interim? What went wrong for him? Two divergent paths to go down in life. When, where did *he* go wrong? I've been working with prisoners for over a decade. It's a troubled life.

I don't happen to know your name. But, you can go back, I think. *You can be that boy again.*

Each of us can. All we have to do is want, and try. And, yes—pray.

In my heart, I hope for him, *You can do it, just try. Just try.*

G-d help him.

And us.

18

Afterword

Emotions are a powerful thing. The most powerful are those that swell up, slowly, over time. They can be sneaky.

On Thursday, June 16, 2005, at exactly five in the afternoon, I retired. I punched the clock—as I had daily for thirteen years—for the last time. But not before I spent my last hour in prison wiping away tears.

Somewhere in mid-2001, I had begun to feel the wear and tear. It is not easy tending to the spiritual needs of grown men in prison. There are high expectations of the chaplain. You are close to heaven. People believe they can always turn to you.

You don't end up in prison without some sort of problem. You don't lose that problem in prison. Usually, it gets worse. Legal problems. Home. Family. Conscience. You need support. You turn to your social worker, ward-officer, cellmate. To the chaplain.

I was there. Exhausted after a forty-plus hour week, I listened. When people depend on you, you find the strength.

It was more than the hours. It was the immediacy. I didn't work on computers—I worked with humans. Someone might say: A real professional is always detached. Maybe. But I still can't hear the real-life stories in this book, directly from the person who's lived them, without being affected.

Things like this would happen. "We got a phone call," my wife, would say. "A summer camp for underprivileged children will be spending the weekend in our village and asked if we had room."

"What did you say?"

"That I'd ask you," she said.

"Miriam, always say we have room."

It wasn't *what* I said—my siblings and I learned an appreciation of having guests in our home while growing up—it was *how*. A bit too sharply.

Let's face it, for thirteen years, I wore a uniform. There's a lot involved in being part of security. There's a mental state. Israel is a country burdened with national security concerns. Each of us has to carry our share of the burden. That's just the way it is.

I took a couple months of unpaid vacation in 2001, again in early 2004.

Don't get me wrong. My salary and benefits were good. I loved the service, and the staff. I still do. Still, I began feeling I might need a change.

As often before, I called my sister, Dr. Elka Pinson, to chew things over. She happens to be a clinical psychologist practicing in Brooklyn, N.Y.

"What you're experiencing," she explained, "is called burnout. There's a library full of professional literature on it. It's not uncommon amongst law enforcement personnel working for extended periods of time in stressful situations."

"And.."

"It's probably time to move on," the doctor said.

In mid-2005, I met with the appropriate committee to ask for an early retirement. My request was granted. Professionals—they'd seen this before.

"You work until the last day of June," I was told by the personnel officer. "Then, you're released." *A civilian, again,* I thought. No more weapons, all-night exercises, military discipline, men looking to me for help.

What's it going to feel like?

On June 16, the personnel officer called me into her office. "We rechecked your unused vacation days. Twenty-two left this year. You have to use them up before release."

"Meaning..."

"Today's your last day," she said.

Today's my last day.

"Enjoy," she said.

It's noon. I have five hours left.

I went back to finish the week as I had so many times. I visited the wards. I distributed supplies from the kitchen to inmates in different wards for their Sabbath cooking. I acted normal.

It was hot and humid and I was sweating.

By four, I finished doing everything I usually did.

How am I supposed to feel? I wasn't really sure.

One hour left.

I made a final pass through Ward B, a place in which I'd invested a lot of time.

I stood alone in the ward synagogue looking out into the hustle and bustle of the prison life.

I remembered an inmate who heard about a disaster at home and cried so hard on my shoulder my shirt was dripping. I had to wait for his body to stop shaking before trying to communicate. Men who shared with me their greatest fears: "My wife wants a divorce." Their greatest joys: "My daughter just finished third grade."

I thought about an outgoing guy who worked with the

maintenance officer, nearing the end of his five year sentence. He drank too much outside, ended up in too many fights. "I'm going back to run my fish restaurant in Tiberia. There's a lot of money in that."

"And..." I said, playfully touching on a point we'd discussed a million times. "Stay away from the booze," he laughed.

I recalled a happy slim guy I liked. I'd taught gym to him—fifteen years back—when he was *eleven*, living in a local orphanage. "You told me I had potential, I should make something of myself," he remembered.

I'd forgotten.

"I hope I will...someday. No one ever said that to me."

No one ever said that to me.

I had a flashback to a talk with an inmate I'd had two weeks ago. Motti, mid-fifties, heavy set, had diabetes, a bad leg and walked with a cane. He always spoke straight.

"I know you believe it's your job to encourage people," he said. *That's true,* I thought. *Though not always as easy as you may think.*

"When you come into the ward, the inmates cheer up. You know what it means for a prisoner when someone smiles, listens, encourages them."

When someone smiles, listens, encourages.

There was another guy, Aaron. His wife, devastated by his incarceration, a charge connected with his accounting firm, called my office regularly. "We're so embarrassed. I want to move. But I'm afraid. I've never sold an apartment. I'll wait for my husband to be released." (He had four years left.) "Thank you for studying with him. You have no idea what that does for him," she whimpered. The line went dead, again.

You have no idea...

I stood looking out over this ward, one of many, I'd tended to for so many years. Many faces had changed. Many had returned. The stories were always the same.

If melancholy is visiting your childhood home, what was the name for leaving such a place?

You don't create such moments. They just happen to you. I believe those sixty minutes were perhaps the most powerful hour of my life. And it opened a crack of light into understanding something I've never understood.

It's something The Rebbe said about a future time. A time many people look forward to. Call it what you may, a new millennium, redemption, a new period. Something he said, I never really got.

The Rebbe believes the world as we know it is progressing

into a new era. This future is described as one of collective and personal prosperity, good will. This concept is common to all major Western faiths, though, frankly, it's based in mine.

What's less known is that reward plays significantly into this picture. Every single good deed, every person you've helped is all there. Nothing is forgotten.

"When that time comes," The Rebbe teaches, "we will all look back, yearning: *I wish I had done more good when I had the chance.*"

I won't say goodbye, I thought. *Not to the inmates, or to other staff.* There'll be too much to say. Too much unsaid.

They'll hear: Jacobs is gone. I'll let it go at that.

Tears flowed down my cheeks. *I came here to change these men.* To take people who've hurt others. Whose actions have shown they believe their fellow man is less important than they are, and to show them compassion is better.

And teach them to stop. Listen to a child's voice. Give some advice, help their fellow man. All said and done, at the end of the day, all we take with us is the good we've done during our lives in this marvelous world given us by the wonderful Creator.

I came to change other men.

But, it was I who changed.

Readers' Guide
Issues for Group Discussion

At various opportunities, the following professionals, and others, discussed the contents of this book. Many ideas arose. Following are a number of issues which they offer for group discussion.

Dr. Elka Pinson, Clinical Psychologist

Dr. Richard Sugarman, Philosophy, University of Vermont

Joseph Jacobs, from a legal perspective

Introduction

Major Jacobs says that the prison service's "overall professional and dignified *modus operandi* applies to all prisoners, without exception." This is meant to include even inmates who have committed horrific crimes.

Is this correct policy for prison authorities, or would stricter codes better serve public interest by helping deter crime?

Major Jacobs accepted the prison service's offer to teach fitness and self-defense to the staff.

How do you feel this influenced the way prisoners and coworkers related to him and, specifically, in his professional role?

The author's using these talents naturally followed the kabbalistic axiom that everything one has—knowledge, possessions, skills—can be utilized in the service of G-d.

Discuss this point. Do you see someone following this principle as being drained of his/her resources? Or, to the contrary, being freed from their innate personal limitations?

Chapter 1 - Ending Up In Jail

In this chapter, the author vividly describes his first day working in prison. The high-powered hustle and bustle in this new environment had an effect on him. "My visceral circuitry," he concludes, "had run an entire gamut, from piqued to frazzled, my nerves numbed from overload." These are experiences not uncommon in high-stress work places.

Have you ever experienced anything similar? Discuss your own experiences which may parallel those described here, and how you dealt with them.

Chapter 2 - Nitzon Prison

This chapter details the true and tragic story of Warden Major Roni Nitzon, who ultimately gave his life in the course of duty. In fact, the rehabilitation and educational programs he sacrificed himself to introduce are changing and saving lives till today.

How do you feel about law-enforcement agents having to confront situations in which their own lives are endangered?

A point from which discussion may begin is the Talmudic wisdom, "Pray for the stability of the government—for without this people would consume one another." What does this mean to emphasize?

Chapter 3 - The Assistant Who Got Canned

Joseph, the new assistant started out as an upbeat, congenial inmate. Slowly, the prison routine drained him—the blow of his twenty-one year sentencing finally broke him. The end of the chapter offers some of his options, but finishes off with, "Whatever he did, the assistant would be doing it alone," and a sad photo of an inmate pacing a yard—all alone.

Imagine yourself in this situation, though not really. You haven't committed any crime. But, you do see yourself in a helpless situation with no out. From where would you draw your strength to continue, to hope?

Chapter 5 - What Would You Say?

This chapter relates the horrifying story of a prisoner who was convicted of murdering his social worker. He subsequently attempted suicide twice. The story ends with his asking, "What can I do to get G-d to forgive me?"

How do you interpret the intention behind his final question, particularly in light of his two attempted suicides?

The author leaves this question in the air. He does not answer. After reading the story, what would you say?

Chapter 6 - What's Your Name?

The narrative here is light, and revolves around an entertaining character. "Sammy was someone I didn't want hanging around our program's classroom unsupervised. He was a graduate of too many army commando units, too strong—220 pounds—and just a bit too 'helpful.' "

Sammy was too "helpful," and needed to be contained. The key was to use intelligence, not force. The story reveals how

Jacobs got Sammy to do what he wanted, without utilizing threats or wasting negative emotion.

Discuss the technique used. How can this, and similar techniques, allow us to get others to cooperate and do as we ask?

Chapter 7 - You Gotta Be Kidding

Here an inmate relates his own escapades which range from possession of a weapon without a license to swindling chain stores out of huge amounts of insurance money. His monologue is transcribed in the casual tone in which it was spoken. It reveals the mindset of someone who is deeply used to crime as a way of life.

Do you believe that anyone—even an seasoned criminal for whom crime has become second nature—can change?

Discuss the differences or parallels that can be drawn between them and everyday people who wish to change undesirable personal traits like anger or jealousy.

Chapter 8 - You Can't Jump To Conclusions

In this chapter, Jacobs observes negotiations between guards and a drugged and violent prisoner. Eventually, things quiet down, the negotiators enter the cell. A commotion erupts, the prisoner needs to be extracted by force. He is injured. But his injuries are actually self-inflicted, though someone who has not seen everything might conclude otherwise.

The chapter concludes that it is not always prudent to form an opinion about something one hasn't personally seen.

Discuss this point, particularly in light of the saying, "Do not judge someone else until you have been in his/her place."

Chapter 10 - Aging With Time

This preamble to the following chapter dissects the self-awareness of criminals at various stages of life, from a youth-related rush of adventure, mellowing in the mid-twenties, to a sobering and rude awakening in the late thirties.

Each of us may be aware of changes in our own perspective on life as the years pass. The Talmud suggests: The youthful years are for plowing and planting, the later are for harvesting.

Discuss how you see this applying to your own life; how and what would you like to be "harvesting."

Chapter 11 - Another Chance

This chapter describes the dilemma of Moshe. It revolves around the following question. Should he request transfer to another prison where he could earn a larger stipend, part of which he'd send to his needy wife, or continue helping the needy inmates in Rabbi Jacobs' prison.

What would you have advised Moshe?

Chapter 13 - A Eulogy

This chapter concludes with a number of people, attending a burial ceremony, eulogizing a convicted criminal. They explain how the deceased, Saul, had tremendously influenced their lives for the good.

How do you feel about their eulogizing a man who spent many years of his life in and out of prison?

The narrative wonders whether Saul helped these individuals on the spur of the moment, to assuage his own conscience, or as a cognitive and measured act.

Discuss this. What is your opinion?

Chapter 15 - *Agunah!*

In this chapter we meet a husband and wife in the throes of a painful divorce. Though Sarah is presently incarcerated, David is no less of a seedy character.

The crux of their battle revolves around child custody.

However, the sorry state of each of these parents does make us think about the larger issues.

Discuss your own views of the relative roles and responsibilities parents have in their children's upbringing.

Chapter 17 - Afterword

The afterword sees the author reflecting back on his thirteen years of service. He relates the thoughts he had during his last emotion laden hour inside prison. Involuntarily, memories of needy inmates whom he has helped pop up into his thoughts.

Rabbi Jacobs ends the book on a hopeful note. "All said and done, at the end of the day, all that we take with us is the good we've done during our lives in this marvelous world given us by the wonderful Creator.

I came to change other men. But, it was I who changed."

Ostensibly, the author means for us to reflect upon these concluding words.

Has this book affected you?

Reference & Bibliography

Photos

Most of the photographs in this book were taken, of course, with permission from the Israel Prison Service. Thanks are extended, again. Like the rest of this book, copyright laws apply to these unless written permission stating otherwise is received from the publisher.

The first photograph on the Contents page is the lock to the maximum security ward in Ayalon Prison where Adolph Eichmann was kept during trial.

The photograph at the end of Chapter 1 shows the author standing at the entrance to Nitzon Prison.

The photograph of Adolph Eichmann was downloaded from *Wikipedia, The Free Encyclopedia.* The disclaimer stated that it had been released into the public domain by the copyright holder, its copyright had expired or it is ineligible for copyright.

The first photograph in Chapter 12 shows the author

instructing prisoners in a classroom within a maximum security prison, the second depicts a more impromptu lesson inside their cell.

The photo at the beginning of the Readers' Guide shows a corridor separating two rows of cells in a typical prison ward.

The other photos of prisoners, either with or without the author, are actual shots taken from the natural location where they occurred. Of course, where applicable, permission was granted.

Introduction

The information regarding Australia, Alcatraz and Sing Sing prisons is found in any number of sources of public knowledge such as numerous popular encyclopedias and online searches.

Dr. Tae Yun Kim has subsequently and successfully trained a number of Olympic competitors, and become a best-selling author, speaker, and CEO.

Chapter 1 - Ending Up In Jail

The information regarding the inmates, present or past, whose names are mentioned in this chapter is taken from public sources of knowledge such as local and international radio broadcasts, Israeli and international newspaper and other media reports and internet searches.

Chapter 2 - Nitzon Prison

The detailed information in this chapter was garnered from newspaper, magazine and other reportings found in the media during that period of time. Due to the nature of that turbulent era, there was extensive coverage during that entire sad episode.

Additionally, Warden Roni Nitzon's parents spoke with me at length and filled in much needed information.

Chapter 9 - Adolph Eichmann

The firsthand descriptions of the Holocaust, from my family members, were heard directly by me. Much of this has been recorded in a, heretofore unpublished, diary written in great detail by my father-in-law.

Besides this, the information in this chapter has been gleaned from many public sources of knowledge, e.g. *Wikipedia, The Free Encyclopedia*, as well as scholarly publications, to name just one: *The Encyclopedia of the Holocaust.* Tel Aviv, Israel, Hebrew edition, Sifriat Poalim Publishing House, 1990.

Chapter 12 - Now You're Talking

The references in this chapter to subjects in Jewish law were taken from the code of law, *Shulchan Aruch Yoreh Deah*, which deals with physical injury and damages.

Chapter 15 - *Agunah!*

The basis of the laws of *agunah* are found in various places in the Talmud and at length in the codes of Jewish law, *Shulchan Aruch.* The strategic decisions, throughout this story, were made in accordance with contemporary legal decisions of the courts presiding over marital disputes. Much of this I had access to through my training as a Rabbinic attorney.

General

In general, I also used a number of professional publications for research. For example, "Viewing the Israel Prison Service," *Ro'im Sha"bos*, a quarterly including excellent scholarly and academic articles. And The Israel Prison Service Annual Report, an official government publication.

The Readers' Guide is intended to provide a starting point

for discussion around issues of general interest raised in this book. And to assist in instructional situations, for example academic settings where subjects such as ethics, philosophy, Israel, criminology, sociology and other social sciences are dealt with.

Web Connections

Israel Prison Service Official Site:

www.ips.gov.il

Links: Neve Tirza Women's' Prison, Marash Hospital, Nitzan Prison, where many of these chapters took place.

Israel Prison Service Unofficial Site:

www.geocities.com/TimesSquare/5432/index.html

Links by author: The Israeli Prison Service Chaplaincy and Religious Wards; A Day in The Life of A Prison Chaplain.

Author's Official Site

www.RabbiJacobs.comπ

Families, particularly children, of inmates have special needs—educational, recreational, social. A portion of the proceeds of book sales will be used to meet these children's needs.

If you would like to help this worthy cause, please send your donation to: Jacobs Media Box 68 383 Kingston Avenue Brooklyn, N.Y. 11213. Make the check payable to Campus Living and Learning Shuls, Inc., a tax-deductible 501 (c) (3) corporation. Note on the check: Free The Children.